Living Traditions

Living Traditions

Half a Millennium of Re-Forming Christianity

Edited by
Kimberlynn McNabb and Robert C. Fennell

RESOURCE *Publications* · Eugene, Oregon

LIVING TRADITIONS
Half a Millennium of Re-Forming Christianity

Copyright © 2019 Wipf and Stock Publishers. All rights reserved. Except for brief quotations in critical publications or reviews, no part of this book may be reproduced in any manner without prior written permission from the publisher. Write: Permissions, Wipf and Stock Publishers, 199 W. 8th Ave., Suite 3, Eugene, OR 97401.

Resource Publications
An Imprint of Wipf and Stock Publishers
199 W. 8th Ave., Suite 3
Eugene, OR 97401

www.wipfandstock.com

PAPERBACK ISBN: 978-1-5326-5979-9
HARDCOVER ISBN: 978-1-5326-5980-5
EBOOK ISBN: 978-1-5326-5981-2

Manufactured in the U.S.A.   APRIL 3, 2019

All Biblical citations in English are from the New Revised Standard Version Bible, copyright © 1989 National Council of the Churches of Christ in the United States of America. Used by permission. All rights reserved.

A version of chapter 7 was previously published as "Tillich for Today's Church: Self-critique, Self-transcendence, and the New Reality" in *Returning to Tillich: Theology and Legacy in Transition*, edited by Russell Manning and Sam Shearn (Berlin: De Gruyter, 2017). Reprinted by permission.

A version of chapter 8 was previously published as "Martin Luther: Late medieval monk and new era revolutionary" in Robert C. Fennell, *The Rule of Faith and Biblical Interpretation: Reform, Resistance, and Renewal* (Eugene, OR: Cascade, 2018). Adapted and reprinted with permission.

Contents

Contributors | vii

Introduction | ix

1   Cherishing the Trees, as Christ is Lord Over All and the Center of All Things | 1
         Martin Luther's Tacit Ecotheological Ethic
           Mark Hubert Lack

2   Unintentional Reformers | 18
         L'Arche, Christian Unity, and the Living Tradition of Footwashing
           Jason Reimer Greig

3   *Ecclesia semper reformanda?* | 31
         Reforming the Church Before, During, and After the Reformation
           Sean A. Otto

4   Most Modern of Churches? | 43
         Charles Taylor and the Baptist Inheritance of the Reformation
           Jesse Smith

5   Living Traditions, A Lutheran Perspective | 52
         Semper Reformanda of *Sola Scriptura, Sola Fide, Sola Gratia*
           Kimberlynn McNabb

6   There's Something About Mary | 61
         How a New Protestant Mariology Can Benefit Ecumenical Dialogue
           Adrienne Findley-Jones

7   Tillich for Today's Church | 76
         The Critique and Gift of the Spiritual Presence
           Andrew O'Neill

8   Luther, the Bible, and the Rule of Faith | 86
       Robert C. Fennell

9   The Intimacy of Trauma | 102
           Musings of a Firefighter Chaplain on Trauma and the Theology of the Cross
           Jeffrey Hosick

10 "If Only—and Yet" | 109
           Luther's Legacy for Jewish-Christian Relations
           Martin Rumscheidt

11 The Death and Resurrection of God | 116
           The Story in a Post-Christian World
           Donald F. Murray

12 Literary Imagination and Theology | 123
           Protestant and Catholic Response to *The Lord of the Rings*
           Allen B. Robertson

Contributors

ROBERT C. FENNELL is Academic Dean and Associate Professor of Historical and Systematic Theology at Atlantic School of Theology. He is author of *The Rule of Faith and Biblical Interpretation: Reform, Resistance, and Renewal* (Eugene, OR: Cascade, 2018).

ADRIENNE FINDLEY-JONES is a doctoral student in theology at Wycliffe College, Toronto. She is studying ethnographic ecclesiology, and Anglican-Lutheran dialogue and relations in the Canadian context.

JASON GREIG is a visiting fellow at the Toronto Mennonite Theological Centre, and completed his PhD at the VU Free University of Amsterdam. Previously, he lived for 11 years at two L'Arche communities in Canada: L'Arche Daybreak and L'Arche Cape Breton.

JEFFREY HOSICK is a veteran firefighter, fire department chaplain, psychotherapist, and professional speaker. His company, LINEOFFIRE.ME, is dedicated to the mental and spiritual health of first responders.

MARK LACK is a professional geoscientist in Mississauga, Ontario, where he has worked for twenty years as an environmental consultant. He recently completed a Master of Theology degree at the University of Toronto.

KIMBERLYNN MCNABB is currently pastor with the people at the Lutheran Church of the Resurrection in Halifax, Nova Scotia. She is also Dean in the Eastern Synod of the Evangelical Lutheran Church in Canada and a sessional instructor at Atlantic School of Theology.

Contributors

Donald F. Murray is a retired minister of The United Church of Canada, educator, workshop facilitator, columnist, and author. He served pastorates in the Maritimes for 32 years and was Program Director and Executive Director at Tatamagouche Centre.

Andrew O'Neill is a minister of The United Church of Canada in Riverview, New Brunswick, and a sessional instructor at Atlantic School of Theology in the fields of theology, ethics, liturgy, and pastoral ministry.

Sean Otto is adjunct faculty at Wycliffe College, University of Toronto. He completed his doctoral dissertation in 2013 on the Latin sermons of John Wyclif. He is currently working on a monograph about Wyclif's antifraternal preaching.

Allen Robertson is an author, historical consultant, and independent scholar with a special interest in the Christian context of J.R.R. Tolkien's writings.

Martin Rumscheidt taught for 27 years at Atlantic School of Theology in the area of historical theology. Since his retirement in 2002, he focuses on the renewal of the relationship between synagogue and church.

Jesse Smith is completing a PhD in systematic theology at St. Paul University, Ottawa, and is a sessional instructor at Atlantic School of Theology.

Introduction

To MARK THE FIVE hundredth anniversary of Martin Luther's posting of his ninety-five theses in 1517—the date conventionally considered to be the start of the European Reformations—Atlantic School of Theology called for papers for a symposium on the ongoing legacies of the many reformations within Christianity that have taken place since that year. As the conveners of that event, we were especially interested to hear a plurality of voices across the ecumenical spectrum, and we were not disappointed. Indeed, the variety of the papers delightfully exceeded our expectations.

Most of the papers given at that event were afterward revised and prepared for the publication you are now reading. Through the perspectives of a firefighter chaplain, geoscientist, history consultant, professors, doctoral students, and clergy—perspectives from a number of denominations, both Protestant and Catholic—we invite you now to explore the continuing influences of the Reformations in life, study, and work. You will find here a range of topics, some of which are not quite what one might expect when considering the streams of thought and ecclesial developments that have flowed since 1517: ecotheology, ecumenism, novels, poetry, trauma, Mariology, footwashing, the nature of the universe, creeds, the Eucharist, human authenticity, Scripture, spiritual presence, polity, and interchurch relations. All of us who have contributed to this volume hope that you will be engaged by this broad spectrum of reflections on the *living traditions* that are still unfolding; that you are intrigued by a novel thought, approach, or application discovered here; and that you are left pondering how the Reformations of half a millennium ago still persist and compel reformation in our own life today.

Introduction

As editors, we would like to thank Atlantic School of Theology for hosting the symposium; all those who attended and presented; and the contributors for their diligent research and writing. We are also grateful to our families for their support, encouragement, and good humour.

KIMBERLYNN MCNABB and ROB FENNELL

1

Cherishing the Trees, as Christ is Lord Over All and the Center of All Things

Martin Luther's Tacit Ecotheological Ethic

Mark Hubert Lack

2017 MARKED THE MAJOR anniversary of more than one publication that has in some way shaped modern thought. Along with the quincentenary of the promulgation of Martin Luther's *Ninety-Five Theses* that set in motion the Protestant Reformation, 2017 also marked the notable anniversary of another seminal document. It was 50 years prior that the historian, Lynn White, famously argued that the earth's environmental crisis stemmed in part from the attitudes and actions of Christians. In an essay published in the journal *Science*, White contended in 1967 that Christianity was the most anthropocentric religion because Christians held that the sole intent of creation was to serve humankind.[1] As a result, this attitude, coupled with humankind's distortion of the divine injunction in the book of Genesis to have dominion over the earth, had contributed to the exploitation and impairment of the natural environment. While Christianity was but one of the contributing factors in White's argument, it was the one that garnered

---

1. White, "Historical Roots."

Living Traditions

all the attention and the one raised repeatedly ever since by environmentalists.² In the past 50 years, have the actions—and inactions—of Christians continued to validate White's charge?

Popular sentiment and scholarly papers alike contend that Christians, particularly evangelicals and "conservative" Protestants,³ are less inclined to support causes that safeguard the environment and the planet's future.⁴ It is felt that evangelical Protestants focus on soteriological and eschatological concerns while disregarding ecological ones, and that they fixate on "heavenly" matters while forsaking earthly ones.⁵ Yet as one scholar observes, a "focus on the afterlife . . . when taken by itself . . . denigrates the creation left behind."⁶

However, Martin Luther, the seminal figure of the Protestant tradition and classic evangelicalism, did not share such an indifference towards the earth. He certainly was no enemy of the environment. As numerous others

---

2. Taylor et al., "Lynn White Jr." Taylor et al. reveal that White's article had 924 citations in the Web of Science's core collection and 4,600 citations in Google Scholar's collection.

3. The terms evangelical and conservative are not necessarily synonymous when describing communities within the Christian faith. In addition, there is not a strict definition for either term that is supported by general consensus. There is ambiguity associated with both terms and diversity within their communities. Nevertheless, I am employing the popular understanding of evangelicals, which I consider to be theologically and socially conservative Protestants.

4. Taylor et al. reference numerous studies that conclude evangelical Christians remain less supportive of environmental issues. Many of these studies are also identified by Djupe and Hunt, "Beyond the Lynn White Thesis" and by Sherkat and Ellison, "Structuring." However, these works also cite reports that indicate the relationship between religion and environmental stewardship is more ambiguous as to where Christianity has exhibited a concern toward the environment. Although organizations such as the Evangelical Environmental Network, the Evangelical Climate Initiative, and countless church-based grass-roots initiatives might suggest that White's indictment is weakening, there remains among some evangelicals hostility towards the environmental movement. See Rudolph, "Evangelical Backlash" and Redden, "Whatever Happened?"

5. Evangelical expectation of the great tribulation to come, Christ's imminent return, and God's promised future restoration of all things has contributed to disregard or at least indifference towards the earth's current environmental condition. In *For the Beauty*, Bouma-Prediger considers some evangelical theological interpretations and how Christianity contributed to the ecological crisis. For a discussion on the possible root of conservative Christianity's failure to promote and preserve the environment, see Northcott, "BP." Dewitt in "Creation's Environmental Challenge" has outlined stumbling blocks that evangelicals have created for themselves that inhibit embracing a reverent attitude and engaging in responsible action towards the environment.

6. Rhoads, "Reflections," 7.

have also suggested from reading Luther, I maintain that the Reformer's theology contains a tacit ecotheological ethic.

Luther's teaching on creation is broad and is scattered throughout his sermons, catechisms, and biblical commentaries. These works reflect his appreciation for the natural world and reveal his understanding of Christ's dominion over it and ubiquitous presence throughout it. Luther viewed the material world as a divine blessing. He did not uphold Platonic philosophy that esteemed the spiritual and denigrated the physical, a view that had greatly influenced medieval Christian theology. The Reformer rejected Gnostic dualism and its view of the inherent evil and inferiority of this temporal domain.[7] Rather, Luther reveled in God's creation and he proclaimed the intrinsic goodness of the sensible world and divine immanence with it. Rightly understood, Luther's theology can therefore contribute to contemporary dialogue with ecology, and perhaps encourage evangelicals—for that matter, all Christians—to respond favorably to the environmental movement and to celebrate the gift of creation, while promoting the sustainable use of its resources.

MANSFELD, MINING, AND THE ENVIRONMENT

Before considering Luther's appreciation of nature and his implicit ecotheological ethic, let us reflect on humankind's exploitation and despoiling of the natural environment in Luther's world. The landscape of sixteenth-century Germany was not pristine. Luther's homeland reflected the effects of many years of mining. Luther would have observed the destructive consequences from the consumption of natural resources. His father, Hans Luther, was a miner and smelting master who operated numerous copper mines and ore smelters around Mansfeld, in the Harz region of Germany.[8]

---

7. Luther's rejection of Platonic idealism is seen foremost in his clash with those who denied the salvific efficacy of Christ's physical body and instead confined it to his spirit. God's incarnation was fundamental to Luther's theology. As such, he countered the teaching of his opponents with "I do not know any God except Him who was made flesh. Nor do I want any other. And there is no other God who could save us besides the God incarnate. Therefore, we shall not suffer His humanity to be underestimated or neglected" (Marburg Colloquy of 1529 in Sasse, *This is My Body*, 203).

8. Hans' surname was actually Luder. Martin had adopted the humanist tradition of using the Hellenized form of his family name, Eleutherios, which he later shortened to Luther.

Living Traditions

Luther's writings make scant mention of his early years, but there is no suggestion that his childhood in the Harz hills was an unhappy one. Still, when the time came, young Martin showed no interest of following in his father's footsteps, admitting years later of his rather limited knowledge of mining.[9] Perhaps the elder Luther also envisioned a future for his son far from the dampness of the mines and the smoke from the smelters. Instead, Martin took up academic studies and left Mansfeld when he was fourteen. Nonetheless, he retained a fondness and a concern for the region and its people his entire life.[10] Luther's lifelong loyalty to Mansfeld is manifested in his advocacy for the area's miners and smelters in their dispute with the Mansfeld nobility who wished to nationalize the mining industry. Although the Reformer may have acknowledged his ignorance regarding the exploration for minerals and the excavation of mines, he was familiar enough with the economics of the industry to believe that nationalization threatened the livelihood of the locals. Cognizant of his mining roots, and all the time exhibiting an affection for Mansfeld, Luther, one of Europe's leading thinkers, late in his life still asserted that he was "ein Mansfeldisch Kind"—a child of Mansfeld.[11]

The roots of mining ran deep in Mansfeld. By the time Hans Luther plied his trade in the Harz Mountains, the region had already been a major mining area for hundreds of years, and a significant source in Europe of silver, copper, and lead. It was during the elder Luther's career that the area underwent phenomenal growth as it rode the mining boom then sweeping the continent. The mid- to late fifteenth century saw an explosion in population across Europe, a period that included Martin Luther's own birth in 1483. With that growth came economic expansion and increased manufacturing, trade, and resource development. The era saw the rise of the modern money-based economy and the corresponding demand for metals. Silver

---

9. As noted in Brecht, *Martin Luther*, 6. As a result of Luther's ignorance of mining he did not incorporate the subject into his sermons as did his friend and one of the transcribers of his *Tischreden*, Johann Mathesius. See Dym, "Mineral Fumes." Following the time he spent at Luther's table, Mathesius became a pastor in Joachimsthal, a significant silver mining region in the Ore Mountains of Bohemia. There Mathesius became friends with George Agricola, the town physician, who was also the author of the pioneering treatise on mining and metallurgy *De re metallica*. Agricola stimulated Mathesius' studies in mining, so much so that Mathesius the mineralogist (rather than the pastor) was recently honored by the scientific community by having a newly discovered mineral named after him. See Plášil, et al., "Mathesiusite."

10. Roper, *Martin Luther*, 17 and Brecht, *Martin Luther*, 9.

11. Luther, "Nr. 4157," 189.

and copper coins were needed to fund commercial trade and everyday transactions—including the payment of papal indulgences. Copper metal was also needed for the printing presses that launched the book publishing industry of the late 1400s. Metal movable type and engraved plates also turned out the certificates of indulgence and, in response, the tracts and treatises that spread the Reformation's teachings.[12] This prodigious demand for metals was met with unprecedented production.[13] New technological developments at the time helped deepen mines, extract more ore, and better refine copper and silver. Yet even with much improved technology, mining was still labor intensive. It is estimated that several thousand laborers worked the mines and stoked the smelters around Luther's hometown in those boom years.[14] During the Reformation, the Mansfeld copper mines, the Upper Harz and Rammelsberg silver workings, and the waterworks that powered them, turned the Harz Mountains into Germany's most industrialized region.[15]

With industrial development came environmental impairment. Mining was energy and water intensive. Large waterwheels powered the machinery that sank the mines, drained the shafts of flooding groundwater, and ventilated them of noxious fumes. This water power also lifted the ore to the surface, crushed the rock with heavy stamps, and washed it of impurities. Muddied and sullied streams now ran off the mountains. Water was then needed to power the bellows and fan the flames that roasted and smelted the ore in furnaces, which belched forth heavy metal-laden smoke. This demand for water meant that in Luther's time a network of

---

12. Pettigrew in *Brand Luther* presents a detailed description of Luther's relationship with the publishing trade and the early printing industry.

13. Almost cotemporaneous with Luther's lifetime (1483-1546), there was a four- to five-fold increase in metal production across Central Europe between 1470 and 1540 (Nef, "Mining and Metallurgy," 755). Roper notes that by the late fifteenth century, Mansfeld was among the largest producers of silver in Europe and produced a quarter of its copper (*Martin Luther*, 17).

14. Nef, "Mining and Metallurgy," 735. Fessner estimates that by 1525 the mining and smelting industry in Mansfeld employed well over 3000 workers. Fessner, "Das Montanwesen," 301. Roper remarks that around this time Hans Luther probably employed about 200 workers in his seven smelting operations (*Martin Luther* 27, 436). This labor force is based on Westermann's estimate that each smelter likely involved 30 workers. Westermann, "Der Wirtschaftliche," 70. Roper also notes that during this period of peak production there were 194 mine shafts around Mansfeld and nearby Eisleben (*Martin Luther* 26).

15. Harzwasserwerke, "UNESCO."

Living Traditions

excavated trenches, rerouted streams, and manmade ponds had begun to spread across the Harz landscape. It was a landscape already littered with shallow pits and slag piles reflecting the hundreds of years of mining and smelting in the region. However, the most significant impact on the environment was the harvesting of timber necessary to produce charcoal to fire the furnaces.[16] The smelters demanded much fuel and the dense hardwood forests of the Harz provided a tremendous resource to be exploited.[17] The deforestation was extensive. Today the name Harz is a misnomer. It had once referred to the thick stands of hardwoods. But beginning in the 1700s, after the harvesting of the oak and beech trees, the region was reforested with softwood spruce trees. The hardwoods were gone.[18]

Martin Luther need not have ventured far to see the environmental consequences of medieval mining. Historian Lyndal Roper notes that from the Luther family house the impacts would have been visible, including the destruction of agricultural lands and a large pond outside the Mansfeld town walls that was contaminated with effluent from the smelters.[19] The town water was largely undrinkable. This is the world Luther grew up in, and yet he loved it.

---

16. An example of forest exploitation in another German mining district during the medieval and early modern era is provided in Tolksdorf et al, "Forest Exploitation."

17. Charcoal was not only produced to fuel the furnaces, but also acted as a chemical agent during the ore smelting process to yield elemental copper. Roper notes that there were 40 smelting masters with operations around Mansfeld in 1508 (*Martin Luther* 24). Like Hans Luther, each master was probably overseeing more than one smelter. An information plaque at Luther's birth house in Eisleben indicates that circa 1500, there were 112 smelting furnaces around Mansfeld, and that they used about 42,000 tonnes of charcoal annually. This volume of consumption would have required about half a million tonnes of timber. Additional quantities of timber were needed to construct the mines and the new mining towns that sprang up in the Harz region.

18. For a discussion on the removal of the hardwoods in the Harz and their replacement with coniferous trees, see Schulz and Jansen, "Study Areas and Basic Data" and Jansen et al., "Modelling."

19. Roper, *Martin Luther*, 20. Roper further indicates that the sixteenth-century historian Cyriacus Spangenberg in his history of Mansfeld (*Mansfeldische Chronica*) provides "a detailed description of the environment, noting that many fields around Mansfeld had been destroyed by mining and . . . the vast quantities of wood and coal used in the mines" (*Martin Luther*, 431n2). Spangenberg (1528-1604) was also a theologian and a pastor in Mansfeld, and was a student of Luther.

LUTHER'S LOVE FOR CREATION AND ITS BEAUTY

Luther had, as Larry Rasmussen describes, "a serious case of 'biophilia,' a love of creaturely life, [as well as] 'cosmophilia,' an utter awe in the presence of life."[20] Luther might have proclaimed that in the gift of creation God richly provides and sustains humankind with all the necessities for earthly life, but besides these practical benefits he pointed out creation's splendor. Although Luther would have witnessed the human impact on the environment, his writings routinely reflect on the beauty and intricacies of the natural world.[21] Whether it is illustrations from the animal kingdom, forests and meadows, or mountains and streams, Luther describes creation as "the most beautiful book."[22] He insists that God has provided humankind "such an attractive dwelling place."[23] Naturally Luther can admire the divine handiwork in the beauty of a rose,[24] but the Reformer even esteemed rodents. He expresses an almost childlike glee when he describes mice as having "a very beautiful form—such pretty feet and such delicate hair . . . [and] therefore here, too we admire God's creation and workmanship."[25] The sixteenth century saw the beginnings of the scientific revolution, and for Luther, the emerging discipline was an opportunity to study more closely the wondrous workings of God's gift of creation.[26] His writings reveal an interest in biology. With the curiosity of a scientist, he observes that if one gazed intently on a kernel of grain "you would die of wonder."[27] Even so, Luther must have had a particular affection for trees. Envisioning a new earth, and perhaps lamenting the loss of the forests on

---

20. Rasmussen, "Waiting for the Lutherans," 93. Bornkamm (*Luther's World*, 185) makes a similar observation and notes that Luther took great pleasure in studying even the most insignificant created works and had an astonishing attention to detail.

21. Schwanke ("Luther on Creation," 1) reminds us that Luther, as a Biblical scholar, developed his doctrine of creation from his study of Genesis, a part of Scripture that the Reformer had a particular fondness for, and on which he wrote and lectured extensively.

22. Luther, cited in Bornkamm, *Luther's World*, 179.

23. *LW* 1:39.

24. Ibid., 54:355.

25. Ibid., 1:52.

26. For a discussion of Luther's view of the emerging sciences in relation to his theology, see Larson, "Martin Luther's Influence."

27. *LW* 36:344.

the Harz hills, he conjectures that the eschatologically restored creation will "be adorned with many trees."[28]

HUMAN IGNORANCE, INDIFFERENCE, AND GREED

Although Luther extolled nature's beauty and phenomena, he recognized that in the Fall, humankind's grasp of and gratitude for creation had been replaced with ignorance, indifference, and greed. He contends that human apathy towards the natural world is in part owing to its familiarity. He suggests that "we do not marvel at the wonderful light of the sun, because it is a daily phenomenon. We do not marvel at the countless other gifts of creation . . . it is a great miracle that a small seed is planted and that out of it grows a very tall oak. But because these are daily occurrences, they have become of little importance."[29] Employing a more visual invective, Luther likens our indifference and ingratitude to the earth's splendor to "cattle . . . trampling the most beautiful blossoms and lilies underfoot."[30]

For Luther, the Fall did not merely result in ignorance or indifference regarding creation. Humankind's distorted state also produced pronounced greed toward God's created blessings. Regarding the beauty of a cherry tree and the thousands of cherries produced from one seed, he rather graphically preaches, "people do not see or heed [it] but pass it by and do [nothing] but gorge and swill all that grows. They are like swine that run across a field or wallow in [the] garden and devour what they find."[31] He further observes that humans "stalk about proudly, act defiantly . . . abusing all the good things and gifts of God only for our own pride, avarice, lust, and luxury."[32] In Luther's view, greed was the manifestation of the sin of idolatry.[33] Greed might express itself as the despoiling of creation and the exploitation of others, but at its core it is rebellion against the Creator. Thus the Reformer

---

28. Ibid., 54:41.

29. Ibid., 1: 126. Likewise, Luther observes human indifference to a hen laying an egg and the birth of a baby chick because it is commonplace, and yet "if we had never seen such an egg and one were brought from Shangri-la, we'd all be startled and amazed." Ibid., 54: 200. Churchill stresses Luther's laments regarding human insensitivity towards natural phenomena and everyday events due to their ubiquity in "'This Lovely Music,'" 183-4.

30. *LW* 54:327.

31. Ibid., 28:179.

32. Luther, "Large Catechism" (*Book of Concord*), 193.

33. Rieth, "Luther on Greed," 163.

considered greed the most dangerous and corrupting force in Christendom.[34] Commenting on the avarice of rich men who plundered the land of tenant farmers in the book of Isaiah, Luther commented that though the world might not rebuke such immoral acts, "God . . . does not want the poor to be thrown off their property but that they be helped."[35]

During the Peasants' War of 1525, Luther might have sided with the German nobility when the rebellious peasants resorted to violence, but he put the blame for the revolt squarely on the shoulders of the princes who had exploited the poor.[36] In a tract entitled *Trade and Usury*, he had earlier expressed his disgust against the exploitative practices of the profit economy. He highlighted the financial houses and trading companies whose manipulative and fraudulent practices he felt oppressed the common people and small businesses.[37] Yet Luther understood that such abuse was not confined to the nobility, the monopolists, or the merchant bankers. He recognized that the emerging market economy presented opportunities for the lower classes to also engage in corrupt and exploitative business practices. According to Luther, thievery in its many forms was "the most common craft and the largest guild on earth."[38]

Observing humankind's insatiable hunger for all things and our disregard for one another's wellbeing, Luther often used the phrase *incurvatus in se*. He contended that we have curved in on ourselves and only seek self-gratification. With the Fall, greed and self-centeredness entered the human heart, distorting humankind's obedience to God's mandate in Genesis to subdue the earth and have dominion over it. Because of this distortion, for many today the word *dominion* in the Genesis context is a pejorative. Luther felt the same way. He acknowledged that "we retain the name and word 'dominion' as a bare title, but the substance itself has been almost entirely lost."[39] Prelapsarian dominion has given way to postlapsarian domination.

In the context of his sixteenth-century understanding, Luther advocated against the abuse of nature, whether it was greed-driven exploitation

---

34. *LW* 21:167.

35. Ibid., 16:61. The comment refers to Isaiah 5:8: "Woe to you who add house to house and join field to field till no space is left and you live alone in the land."

36. Ibid., 46:17-43.

37. Ibid., 45:244-308. For a discussion of Luther's understanding of usury and the emerging market economy, see Lindberg, "'Christianization.'"

38. Luther, "Large Catechism" (*Concordia Triglotta*), 417. This is his commentary on the Seventh Commandment.

39. *LW* 1:67.

or malicious destruction. In his commentary on Genesis, Luther appreciates that God has provided us with the riches of the earth to enjoy, but we are to do so "in proportion to [our] need."[40] Along with encouraging modest consumption of nature's resources, Luther's writings also appear to promote nature's protection. For example, trees are not to be ravaged but safeguarded. He likened the springtime blossoming of trees to our own glorious resurrection and the coming restoration of all things. Thus he contends that when "Christians look at [trees] they do not think of gormandizing like swine; no, in them they see the work prefigured which God will perform on us."[41] Even during warfare the earth was to be respected: Luther expected that invading armies not cut down the trees of their enemies, "not to devastate a land which has not sinned."[42] If they do, Luther avowed that the sinless land does not suffer silently. He observes even an innocent tree "that is cut down does not tumble to the ground without a creaking noise."[43]

In many of his reflections regarding creation, Luther invoked Christ—the sinless one who suffered silently—and it is Christ that we now consider.

CHRIST'S DOMINION, IMMANENCE, AND UBIQUITY

While he contends that humankind has "dominion" in bare title only, Luther also proclaims who has true dominion. True dominion is only acquired through holiness, and thus it lies with Christ alone.[44] For Luther, "it is Christ the Lord, who was present at the time of creation of all things not as a mere spectator but as a coequal Creator and Worker, who still governs and preserves all and will continue to govern and preserve all until the end of the world."[45] By asserting that it is Christ who has dominion over all, Luther has now a new and deeper appreciation for creation. Thus he declares,

---

40. Ibid., 1:39. Churchill emphasizes Luther's limitation in "'This Lovely Music,'" 195.

41. *LW* 28:180.

42. Ibid., 9:204.

43. Ibid., 13: 107. This audible response to suffering is reminiscent of the groaning of creation in Romans 8. Walsh et al. present a thoughtful study on "hearing the voices of creation," particularly those of trees that suffer abuse. In proposing a reciprocal relationship between trees and humans, they consider the responsive nature of trees, scientifically, and scripturally. Walsh, "Trees, Forestry." Stewart ("Heaven Has No Sorrow") presents an imaginative discussion of the ecological suffering of creation at human hands in Scripture as an approach to encouraging an emotion-based environmental ethic.

44. *LW* 11:393. Luther's contention is derived from his exposition of Psalm 114:2.

45. Ibid., 22:28.

"Now if I believe in God's Son and bear in mind that He became man, all creatures will appear a hundred times more beautiful to me than before. Then I will properly appreciate the sun, the moon, the stars, trees, apples, and pears, as I reflect that He is Lord over all and the Center of all things."[46]

While affirming Christ's transcendent lordship, Luther is nevertheless also always aware of his immanent presence. Christ has dominion over creation, but he is also present throughout it. Thus, the Reformer was wont to say: Christ "is, with, and under" all things. Luther's awareness of divine immanence and Christ's ubiquitous presence in creation is forcefully expounded in his debate with fellow reformer, Ulrich Zwingli, regarding Christ's real presence in the Eucharist. This is a crucial point in our discussion and one that is presented in the work of numerous Lutheran theologians, including Paul Santmire and Cynthia Moe-Lobeda. These scholars have observed in Luther's eucharistic theology, and in his affirmation of the created world's goodness, a tacit ecotheological ethic that invites amplification.

Zwingli had argued that since the ascended Christ is now at the right hand of the Father, he cannot be present locally in the creaturely elements of bread and the wine. However, Luther countered that Christ was truly present in the Eucharist. He expounded:

> the right hand of God is not a specific place . . . such as . . . a golden throne, but [it] is the almighty power of God, which at one and the same time can be nowhere and everywhere . . . essentially present at all places, even in the tiniest leaf . . . [God] himself must be present in every single creature in its innermost and outermost being, on all sides, through and through, below and above, before and behind.[47]

As we see in his description of the divine presence within and throughout creation, Luther used a variety of prepositions and this, as Santmire contends, protects the Reformer against assertions of panentheism.[48] God was not merely 'in' the creature, but also above it, below it, and with it. Nor was Luther a pantheist. He always maintained the Creator-creature distinction. God is not the creature nor can he be contained within it.[49] For Luther, the

---

46. Ibid., 496.
47. Ibid., 37:57-8.
48. Santmire, "Creation and Salvation," 184.
49. Santmire, *Before Nature*, 141. Similarly, Westhelle ("The Weeping Mask," 145) relates that for Luther, "God is *in* creation without being creation."

Creator is always immediately present with creation, but he is also always separate from it and transcendent to it. As Santmire observes, for Luther, "our commonplace spatial categories simply do not apply to God."[50] The Reformer recognized that divine transcendence and immanence was a mystery. Yet although he acknowledged that these were "exceedingly incomprehensible matters," Luther believed they were attested in Scripture.[51] Citing Jeremiah 23:23-24, Luther understood that God is both nearby and far off, and fills heaven and earth.[52]

Christ's eucharistic presence gave Luther the platform to proclaim divine immanence and ubiquity, and in turn gives contemporary theologians the occasion to observe in the Reformer an ecotheological ethic. Such an ethic can in turn provide further motive to respect and preserve the natural world, without idolatrizing it. As Moe-Lobeda offers, "if, as Luther asserts, God dwells not only in human creatures but also in all earth's bounty, then . . . God's presence there . . . obligate[s] us to live toward the healing and sustaining of creation."[53]

CARING FOR CREATION AS FELLOW WORKERS WITH CHRIST

Although Luther's theological teachings initiated reform of the ecclesiastical abuses perpetrated by the papacy five hundred years ago, his teachings can also encourage reform of the ecological abuses committed by Christians today. Luther may have gazed upon the natural world with wonder, but at the same time, he mined Scripture to defend divine immanence in that natural world and to proclaim Christ's dominion over it. These explicit pronouncements reflect a tacit ecotheological ethic that can rouse Christians to engage environmental concerns. Yet within Luther there remains a further incentive: God desires that human beings participate with him in tending to creation.

---

50. Santmire, *Before Nature*, 139.
51. *LW* 37:59.
52. Luther, "Confession," 266.
53. Moe-Lobeda, "Journey," 422. Bayer also relates that because of our planet's "ecological crisis, it becomes increasingly necessary to speak theologically about the immanence of God in the world" (*Martin Luther's Theology*, 103. Similarly, Churchill highlights Luther's eucharistic theology and divine immanence to promote an ecotheological ethic ("'This Lovely Music,'" 187-8).

Lack—Cherishing the Trees

There is an anecdote (perhaps apocryphal) that relates how Luther, when asked what he would do if he knew that the world would end tomorrow, is alleged to have replied, "I would still plant my apple tree."[54] In his essay on Luther's ethics, Gerhard Forde understands the story to imply that when all is said and done, and the Kingdom of God has come, Luther believed that God should find us doing what he intended of us: "taking care of creation."[55] For Luther, our calling from God, our vocation, whether sacred or secular, great or small, goes hand in hand with ethics.[56] We fulfill this hand in hand with God in Christ. Luther reminds his readers of their role of collaborating with the Creator, who "does not work in us without us, because it is for this he has created and preserved us, that he might work in us and we might cooperate with him."[57] Thus in the divine work of preserving and sustaining creation, God enlists and enables humankind to become fellow workers with Christ and earthly agents of his healing.[58]

If Luther is correct that God has given humankind the privilege of collaborating with Christ in his dominion, evangelicals are provided with the impetus to embrace and safeguard their earthly home. However, Luther would be the first to remind Christians that the ethical act of stewarding creation—or any ethical act, for that matter—in no way justifies one before God. The Reformer proclaimed that one's reconciliation with the Creator is solely based on Christ's salvific work and his righteousness, which God graciously bestows on his people. This is the crux of the Reformation. Justification by faith in Christ's work frees the Christian from attempting to

---

54. Luther's declaration might partly reflect his affection for trees, but as Hendrix relates, the statement has not been found in any of the Reformer's writings. Hendrix further indicates that scholars have attributed the anecdote to the German Confessing Church to inspire resistance against the Nazis during World War II. Hendrix, *Martin Luther*, 90.

55. Forde, "Luther's Ethics," 149.

56. Ibid., 148.

57. *LW* 33:243. While Schwanke notes Luther's frequent emphasis on the divine seeking human cooperation, Gregersen particularly references the quote cited above and applies this example of Luther's understanding of human participation with God to the preservation of creation. See Schwanke, "Luther on Creation," 7 and Gregersen, "Grace," 24.

58. Rasmussen and Moe-Lobeda ("The Reform Dynamic," 138) also emphasize that Christ works with human beings in restoring creation, based on Luther's statement that Christ "is present in the sacrament and in the hearts of believers not really because he wants to be worshipped there, but because he wants there to work with us and help us." *LW* 36:294.

justify oneself by one's own work. Instead, now empowered by the Spirit, the Christian responds to God's grace by freely serving his people and "saving the planet." As Kolb and Arand observe, "faith in the God who justifies is at the same time faith in the God who created the world [and] thus, faith embraces the world as God's good creation."[59] Evangelicals who rightly admire and assert Luther's teaching on justification ought also to endorse his ethic that upholds creation and denounces its abuse.

CONCLUSION

Fifty years ago, Lynn White argued that Christian arrogance had led to an ecological crisis. For White, the root of the problem was a religious one, but he also believed—and probably to the chagrin of non-Christian environmentalists—that the solution was religious. Thus White encouraged Christians to consider Saint Francis of Assisi, who was a friend to all creatures and whom White called "the greatest spiritual revolutionary since Christ."[60] By doing so, White hoped to highlight both Francis's humble, reverent attitude toward creation and his convictions about humankind's non-domineering place within it. White concluded his essay by proposing that Francis be considered the "patron saint of ecologists."[61] I will conclude by proposing that another revolutionary, Luther, also share that honor.

BIBLIOGRAPHY

Bayer, Oswald. *Martin Luther's Theology: A Contemporary Interpretation*. Translated by Thomas H. Trapp. Grand Rapids: Eerdmans, 2008.

Bornkamm, Heinrich. *Luther's World of Thought*. Translated by Martin H. Bertram. Saint Louis: Concordia, 1958.

Bouma-Prediger, Steven. *For the Beauty of the Earth: A Christian Vision of Creation Care*. Grand Rapids: Baker Academic, 2010.

Brecht, Martin. *Martin Luther, Volume 1: His Road to Reformation, 1483-1521*. Translated by James L. Schaaf. Philadelphia: Fortress, 1985.

Churchill, Steven L. "'This Lovely Music of Nature': Grounding an Ecological Ethic in Martin Luther's Creation Mysticism." *Currents in Theology and Mission* 26, no. 3 (June 1999): 183-95.

---

59. Kolb and Arend, *Genius*, 106.
60. White, "Historical Roots," 1206.
61. Ibid., 1207.

Dewitt, Calvin. "Creation's Environmental Challenge to Evangelical Christianity." In *The Care of Creation: Focusing Concern and Action*, edited by R.J. Berry, 60-73. Leicester, England: InterVarsity, 2000.

Djupe, Paul A., and Patrick K. Hunt. "Beyond the Lynn White Thesis: Congregational Effects on Environmental Concern," *Journal for the Scientific Study of Religion* 48, no. 4 (Dec 2009): 670-86.

Dym, Warren. "Mineral Fumes and Mining Spirits: Popular Beliefs in the *Sarepta* of Johann Mathesius (1504-1565)." *Renaissance and Reformation Review* 8, no. 2 (Mar 2006): 161-85.

Fessner, Michael. "Das Montanwesen in der Grafschaft Mansfeld vom ausgehenden 15. bis zur zweiten Hälfte des 16. Jahrhunderts." In *Montanregion als Sozialregion*, edited by Angelika Westermann, 293-320. Matthiesen Verlag, 2012.

Forde, Gerhard O. "Luther's Ethics." In *A More Radical Gospel: Essays in Eschatology, Authority, Atonement, and Ecumenism*, edited by Gerhard O. Forde, Mark C. Mattes, and Steven D. Paulson, 137-41. Grand Rapids: Eerdmans, 2004.

Gregersen, Niels Henrik. "Grace in History and Nature: Luther's Doctrine of Creation Revisited." *Dialog: A Journal of Theology* 44, no. 1 (Spring 2005): 19-29.

Harzwasserwerke. "UNESCO-Welterbe Oberharzer Wasserwirtschaft, Die Anlagen des Oberharzer Wasserregals." Marz 2011. http://www.harzwasserwerke.de/fileadmin/user_upload/downloads/files/pdf/Flyer/Flyer_UNESCO-Welterbe-Oberharzer-Wasserwirtschaft.pdf. Accessed 6 April 2017.

Hendrix, Scott H. *Martin Luther: A Very Short Introduction*. Oxford: Oxford University Press, 2010.

Jansen, M., and W. Schmidt, V. Stüber, H. Wachter, C. Naeder, M. Weckesser, and F.J. Knauft. "Modelling of Natural Woodland Communities in the Harz Mountains." In *Spatial Modelling in Forest Economy and Management: A Case Study*, edited by M. Jansen, M. Judas, and J. Saborowski, 162-75. Berlin: Springer, 2002.

Kolb, Robert, and Charles P. Arand. *The Genius of Luther's Theology: A Wittenberg Way of Thinking for the Contemporary Church*. Grand Rapids: Baker Academic, 2008.

Larson, Duane H. "Martin Luther's Influence on the Rise of the Natural Sciences." *Oxford Research Encyclopedia of Religion* (Nov 2016). http://religion.oxfordre.com/view/10.1093/acrefore/9780199340378.001.0001/acrefore-9780199340378-e-306. Accessed 6 April 2017.

Lindberg, Carter. "'Christianization' and Luther on the Early Profit Economy." In *The Reformation as Christianization: Essays on Scott Hendrix's Christianization Thesis*, edited by Anna Marie Johnson and John A. Maxfield, 49-78. Tübingen: Mohr Siebeck, 2012.

Luther, Martin. "Confession Concerning Christ's Supper – From Part I (1528)." In *Martin Luther's Basic Theological Writings*, 2nd ed., edited by Timothy F. Lull, 262-79. Minneapolis: Augsburg, 2005.

———. "The Large Catechism." In *The Book of Concord: The Confessions of the Evangelical Lutheran Church*, edited by Robert Kolb and Timothy J. Wengert, translated by Eric Gritsch and Charles P. Arand. Minneapolis: Fortress, 2000.

———. "The Large Catechism." In *Concordia Triglotta: The Symbolical Books of the Evangelical Lutheran Church*, edited and translated by F. Bente and W.H.T. Dau. Saint Louis: Concordia, 1922.

———. *Luther's Works*. 55 vols. Edited by Jaroslav Pelikan et al. American Edition. Philadelphia: Muehlenberg and Fortress, 1955-86.

———. *D.Martin Luthers Werke. Kritische Gesamtausgabe. Tischreden*. 2. Band. Weimar: Hermann Böhlaus Nachfolger, 1913.

———. "Nr. 4157, Luther an die Grafen Philipp and Johann Georg von Mansfeld, Mansfeld, 7. Oktober 1545." In *D. Martin Luthers Werke. Kritische Gesamtausgabe. Briefwechsel* 11. Band. Weimar: Hermann Böhlaus Nachfolger, 1948.

Moe-Lobeda, Cynthia. "Journey between Worlds: Economic Globalization and Luther's God Indwelling Creation." *Word and World* 21, no. 4 (Fall 2001): 413-23.

Nef, John U. "Mining and Metallurgy in Medieval Civilisation." In *The Cambridge Economic History of Europe Volume II: Trade and Industry in the Middle Ages*, 2nd ed., edited by M.M. Postan and Edward Miller, 691-761. Cambridge: Cambridge University Press, 1987.

Northcott, Michael S. "BP, the Blowout and the Bible Belt: Why Conservative Christianity Does Not Conserve Creation." *The Expository Times* 122, no. 3 (Dec 2010): 117-26.

Pettegree, Andrew. *Brand Luther*. New York: Penguin, 2015.

Plášil, Jakub, František Veselovský, Jan Hloušek, Radek Škoda, Milan Novák, Jiří Sejkora, Jiří Čejka, Pavel Škácha, and Anatoly V. Kasatkin, "Mathesiusite, $K_5(UO_2)_4(SO_4)_4(VO_5)(H_2O)_4$, A New Uranyl Vanadate-Sulfate from Jáchymov, Czech Republic." *American Mineralogist* 99, no. 4 (2014): 625-32.

Rasmussen, Larry. "Waiting for the Lutherans." *Currents in Theology and Mission* 37, no. 2 (April 2010): 86-98.

Rasmussen, Larry, and Cynthia Moe-Lobeda. "The Reform Dynamic: Addressing New Issues in Uncertain Times." In *The Promise of Lutheran Ethics*, edited by Karen L. Bloomquist and John R. Stumme, 131-50. Minneapolis: Fortress, 1998.

Redden, Molly. "Whatever Happened to the Evangelical-Environmental Alliance?" *The New Republic* (3 Nov 2011). https://newrepublic.com/article/97007/evangelical-climate-initiative-creation-care. Accessed 19 Nov 2018.

Rieth, Ricardo Willy. "Luther on Greed." In *Harvesting Martin Luther's Reflections on Theology, Ethics, and the Church*, edited Timothy J. Wengert, 152-68. Grand Rapids: Eerdmans, 2004.

Rhoads, David. "Reflections on a Lutheran Theology of Creation: Foundations for a New Reformation." *Seminary Ridge Review* 15, no. 1 (Fall 2012): 8.

Roper, Lyndal. *Martin Luther: Prophet and Renegade*. London: Bodley Head, 2016.

Rudolph, John Collins. "An Evangelical Backlash Against Environmentalism." *The New York Times* (30 December 2010).

Santmire, H. Paul. *Before Nature: A Christian Spirituality*. Minneapolis: Fortress, 2014.

———. "Creation and Salvation according to Martin Luther: Creation as the Good and Integral Background." In *Creation and Salvation Volume 1: A Mosaic of Selected Classical Christian Theologies*, edited by Ernest M. Conradie, 173-202. Berlin: Lit Verlag, 2012.

Sasse, Hermann. *This is My Body: Luther's Contention for the Real Presence in the Sacrament of the Altar*. Adelaide: Lutheran, 1977.

Schulz, R. and M. Jansen. "Study Areas and Basic Data." In *Spatial Modelling in Forest Economy and Management: A Case Study*, edited by M. Jansen, M. Judas, and J. Saborowski, 11-18. Berlin: Springer, 2002.

Schwanke, Johannes. "Luther on Creation." Translated by John Betz. *Lutheran Quarterly* 16 (2002): 1-20.

Sherkat, Darren E., and Christopher G. Ellison. "Structuring the Religion-Environment Connection: Identifying Religious Influences on Environmental Concern and Activism." *Journal for the Scientific Study of Religion* 46, no. 1 (Mar 2007): 71-85.

Stewart, Alexander Coe. "Heaven Has No Sorrow that Earth Cannot Feel: The Ethics of Empathy and Ecological Suffering in the Old Testament." *Canadian Theological Review* 4 no. 2 (2015): 19-34.

Taylor, Bron, Gretel Van Wieren, and Bernard Daley Zaleha, "Lynn White Jr. and the Greening-of-Religion Hypothesis." *Conservation Biology* 30, no. 5 (Apr 2016): 1000-09.

Tolksdorf, Johann Friedrich, Rengert Elburg, Frank Schröder, Hannes Knapp, Christoph Herbig, Thorsten Westphal, Birgit Schneider, Alexander Fülling, Christiane Hemker, "Forest Exploitation for Charcoal Production and Timber Since the 12th Century in an Intact Medieval Mining Site in the Niederpöbel Valley (Erzgebirge, Eastern Germany)." *Journal of Archeological Science: Reports* 4 (Dec 2015): 487-500.

Walsh, Brian J., Marianne B. Karsh, and Nik Ansell, "Trees, Forestry, and the Responsiveness of Creation." *Cross Currents* 44, no. 2 (Sum 1994): 149-62.

Westhelle, Vitor. "The Weeping Mask: Ecological Crisis and the View of Nature." *Word and World—Theology for Christian Ministry* 11, no. 2 (Spr 1991): 137-46.

Westermann, Ekkehard."Der Wirtschaftliche Konzentration-prozess im Mansfelder Revier." In *Martin Luther und der Bergbau im Mansfelder Land: Aufsätze*, edited by Rosemarie Knape. Stiftung Luthergedenkstätten in Sachsen-Anhalt, 2000.

White, Lynn Jr. "The Historical Roots of Our Ecologic Crisis." *Science* 155, no. 3767 (March 1967): 1203-7.

2

Unintentional Reformers

L'Arche, Christian Unity, and the Living Tradition of Footwashing

Jason Reimer Greig

THE CHURCH OF CHRIST is divided. The body that Jesus prays "may be one" is persistently and stubbornly fragmented. This is a scandal for the church and impedes its mission to witness to God's peace and unity in the world. The question becomes, what do we do about it? Can we do anything? Does it really matter all that much? Do we just accept it and move on? If, like me, you actually believe in visible unity, do you join me and futilely fume over ecclesial intransigence, or dream of some future impossible reality? Is there any sign of unity even possible in our world?

In this chapter, I argue that the impasse of Christian unity today emanates from key ideas and events of the late medieval Reformation and the early modern period. Drawing on Brad Gregory's book, *The Unintended Reformation*, I will show how, among other things, the loss of a vision of substantive moral community, which ensued from the Reformation, privatized faith, and led to a subjectivized, individualistic ethic, incommensurate with the unification of the church. I will then argue that the communities of L'Arche represent an international manifestation of local subcultures, able to unify people across wide forms of difference in a common faith and way of life. One sacramental practice the church might take from L'Arche as a guide and way to unity is that of footwashing. Footwashing demonstrates

L'Arche's orientation to friendship with God and the other that builds up the body and makes a space for deep encounter and dialogue.

THE UNINTENDED REFORMATION

In *The Unintended Reformation*, Brad Gregory embarks on an ambitious project not only to interpret the history of the Reformation period, but also to trace the core of this event in contemporary Western culture. Gregory begins by pointing out three markers of contemporary US culture, which he understands as all having their source in the late Middle Ages and early modern periods.[1] The first marker is the ever-increasing degree of polarization evident in US society. The growing divide between urban-rural, right-left, ultra-rich-dirt-poor (or whichever dichotomy one wants to name) seems to know no end. Accompanying this polarization is an oftentimes intense shrillness in public debate, which only further alienates sides from each another. The second aspect of contemporary culture Gregory highlights is the reality of climate change and its link with gross forms of consumerism. Global capitalism's incessant need for growth requires citizens to be formed in a consumerist mindset. The quantity of consumption this worldview requires only exacerbates climate change, and often directly contradicts personal, local, and national efforts at reducing ecological footprints. A third marker of US culture is the questioning, if not outright denial, of any objective basis for truth, as a consequence of late modern hyperpluralism. In this assumed realm of moral relativism, morality loses its grounding in truth, and becomes the created norms of those with power. People still need the moral categories of "good" and "bad," but without a solid ground on which to base them, why would any of us deem them true?[2]

After discerning these three dimensions of late modernity in the US, Gregory then moves to the core of his argument. According to Gregory, the Reformation period saw the end of an institutionalized worldview based on virtue and its cultivation in practices of the church. This worldview came to an end because of the large gap between the church's prescriptions and the corruption inside the church itself, most scandalously in its leaders.

---

1. Gregory, *Unintended Reformation*, 15-20.

2. Although these have occurred after Gregory's book, one only needs to think of the emergence of "post-fact" or "post-truth" assertions to see the trajectory of moral relativity.

Living Traditions

The Reformers' belief in renewal through a more correct interpretation of doctrine, grounded on *sola scriptura*, unintentionally created endless conflict, not just with the church centered in Rome, but also amongst the Reformers themselves. Secular rulers were increasingly impatient with this intra-ecclesial animosity, especially when it spilled out into violent conflicts. Enlightenment philosophers attempted an answer to the dilemma by enshrining objective, scientific reason as true knowledge, in turn pushing religion and its knowledge to the private sphere. At the same time, secular states saw the Dutch Republic's consumption-centered economy as the palliative to destructive religious disagreement. When the promise of undergirding knowledge on reason alone—a kind of *sola ratio*—began to break up, enlightened self-interest through consumption appeared to be one of the few things holding Western societies together. The cohesiveness of the system was illusory, based on an individualism that removed truth from the public square and ensconced it in the legal rights of alienated persons. This schema ultimately fared poorly in uniting persons around a common good because it preferred a center based on the *goods life* to that of the *good life*. Such an anthropology and epistemology became enshrined in the growing power of secular universities, aided through the confessionalization of education.

THE LOSS OF SUBSTANTIVE MORAL COMMUNITY

Gregory's extended argument is based on six key theses or narratives. I will focus on the fourth. The basic claim Gregory wishes to develop here is how disagreement over the good, produced through proliferating truth claims, displaced a common teleological ethic for a subjectivized one based on the protection of individual rights. A fundamental part of Gregory's argument is his claim that medieval Europe was undergirded by an institutionalized worldview, which had a shared moral vision based in a kind of Christian virtue ethic. This does not mean that Gregory sees the Middle Ages as a kind of monolithic age, where everyone moved lockstep with the dictates of the church. Gregory interprets history with nuance, seeing "The late medieval church [as] a large playground, but one enclosed by forbidding fences—an almost riotous diversity held together in an overarching unity by a combination of ingrained customs, myriad institutions, varying degrees of self-conscious dedication, and the threat of punishment."[3] A unifying aspect of

3. Ibid., 84.

society consisted of a morality which upheld a common end, namely, "to live as part of the body of Christ extended in space and time—the moral community of the church, including its deceased members militant and triumphant—through the shared practice of the virtues constitutive of that community as the *via* to salvation."[4]

The church's own failure to practice virtue, especially among its leaders, created an enmity that drove some to reform and start again. While not all the Reformers wished to eliminate a more traditional teleological ethic, the virulence of the disagreement that followed began to erode credibility in any kind of Christian morality. Added to this doubt was the creation of confessionally separate ecclesial bodies. As Gregory explains, "The constitution of mutually exclusive moral communities would eventually suggest to some people that morality itself is contingent and constructed, or at least that its basis and precepts are separable from religion."[5] Gregory makes the important point that this move toward autonomous ecclesial communities, impelled by intense doctrinal agreement, had profound social implications. Because moral communities are inescapably social, the bitter feuding amongst competing interpretations could only assist in fragmenting the organic solidarity built up through a broad commitment to a common institutionalized worldview.[6]

The religious wars of the modern period did not help matters. The increasing power of secular authorities (and the eventual development of the state) led to the granting of "religious freedom" to the individual conscience, resulting in what Gregory sees as a tremendous shift in morality. "Because *individuals* disagreed about the meaning of God's word, *individuals* and not politically favored churches were and had to be the bearers of rights, beginning with the right to religious liberty . . . This meant that individuals had simultaneously been conceived—in principle—as their own arbiters of the good, because the good is exactly what is at stake in the disagreements among Christians."[7] The ground for morality, thus, went from substantive communities of virtue to individual "authentic" subjects.

While Gregory only quotes him overtly a few times, moral philosopher Alasdair MacIntyre's virtue ethic remains "deep background" in *The*

---

4. Ibid., 195.
5. Ibid., 204-5.
6. Ibid., 203-6.
7. Ibid., 215-6.

Unintended Reformation.⁸ Gregory (at least implicitly) laments the loss of a virtue based, common worldview of the Middle Ages, and sees the resultant individualistic, consumerist ethic that follows as deeply destructive for Western society in particular and globally in general. Nowhere does Gregory call for a return to a bygone golden age, or even advocate for MacIntyre's morality of virtue.⁹ As an historian, Gregory makes the much less grandiose suggestion that (secular) universities open themselves up to religious reasoning as an equally legitimate form of knowledge. Yet one still picks up echoes of the desire to see what a community of the "new Benedict" might look like in the late modern West, and what it might do to recover a morality both Christian and public for today.¹⁰

I suggest that the communities of L'Arche might just represent such a type of reformed community, which not only helps form persons in a teleological ethic, but also acts as a sign of what visible ecclesial unity might look like. L'Arche communities may unintentionally prove to look and act a great deal like MacIntyre's "new Benedict," doing this not primarily through theological commissions, but through sharing life together as friends of God and one another.

GOD'S PROJECT: L'ARCHE AS A PARABLE OF UNITY

The beginning of L'Arche happened simply and harmlessly enough. Jean Vanier, former naval officer, recent university graduate, and son of former Canadian diplomat and Governor General Georges Vanier welcomed three men from a local institution to live with him in a small home in the French village of Trosly-Breuil.¹¹ Called by God to form community with persons confined to institutional life, Vanier gradually welcomed more persons in homes in the village, and L'Arche began to expand quickly. These new homes also needed nondisabled people in them, many of them arriving through word of mouth.

Vanier found a common thread among many of the nondisabled newcomers: a desire to live an authentic Christian faith in the context of intentional community. This was the 1960s, with its countercultural impulses

---

8. MacIntyre, *After Virtue*.

9. Note the subtitle to Gregory's conclusion: "Against Nostalgia."

10. MacIntyre, *After Virtue*, 263.

11. On the history and interpretation of L'Arche, see Vanier, *Ark for the Poor* and *Our Life Together*; Spink, *The Miracle*.

and an awakening to the destructive dimensions of modern life. Vanier readily saw and affirmed the desire of many to live and work for a more liberated world, especially for those most oppressed and marginalized.

There was a clear difference between L'Arche and many other attempts at intentional community. It lay in a very concrete common goal: living in relationship with people labeled intellectually disabled. The needs of many of these persons were quite evident and required the embodied presence and attention of nondisabled assistants in an immediate way. The life sharing that ensued led Vanier and others to the realization that L'Arche must mean far more than mere do-goodery, but instead was centered in a transformative realization that those with cognitive impairments were teaching the nondisabled about faith, life, and being human. In short, persons labeled as disabled were becoming not "patients" or "clients," but *friends*. Although community life was often messy and anything but ideal, the conversions experienced in L'Arche—both for those considered disabled and for the nondisabled—convinced Vanier and others that the movement was truly "God's project."[12]

In part, this transformation occurred because Vanier had instilled a particular theological anthropology within L'Arche's social imaginary. Vanier's personal convictions were founded on a solid belief in every human person being made in the image of God, and at the same time, made for being in relationship with others. Community, as much as (or even more than) individual freedom, stood as fundamental for persons. Friendship, grounded in the human *telos* as friendship with God, stood as a key moral relation and ground for communal unity. This is how Vanier understood L'Arche's need to anchor itself relationally because he saw persons considered disabled as needing far more than good care. What they really wanted were true relationships of friendship, a common human need recognized since Aristotle as the relation that most unites the *polis*.[13]

Friendship occurs in community, where persons grow on their journey of faith to God, and where members are nurtured and formed in the communities' particular virtues and practices. The goal of this formation

---

12. Vanier, *Ark for the Poor*, 16.

13. Vanier's Aristotelian training had attuned him to friendship as that relation that builds unity within the social body. See Vanier, *Made for Happiness*, 170. Vanier continually discovered this reality sharing life together with persons labelled as intellectually disabled as well as those considered nondisabled. On his observations of friendship as a basic human need, especially for those with cognitive impairments, see *Ark for the Poor*, 57 and *Community and Growth*, 97.

is not to produce identical automatons, but rather to valorize difference as a gift given for communion. "Unity is achieved when each member of the body is different and contributes a different gift, but are all united around the same goal, by mutual love."[14] The end result of community, Vanier continually reiterates, should not look like a pyramid but a body.[15] When the church is living her vocation authentically, it will take seriously Paul's words about the weak and poor as being indispensable to that body.

L'ARCHE AND ECUMENISM

It was on these foundations of God's friendship, and friendship with the marginalized, that L'Arche's ecumenical history and vocation was based. Vanier had no indication that L'Arche, as a child of 1960s France, would be anything more than a small Roman Catholic community. Yet the desire to form L'Arche in ecumenical Canada and interfaith India faced the movement with another reality. After much reflection, Vanier chose, in disagreement with his Dominican spiritual father, to let the Holy Spirit lead L'Arche into ecumenical and interfaith waters, an inspired pragmatism that continues to this day.

Based on an orientation to persons over structure, and friendship with the other over community with the like-minded, L'Arche let God lead it into its ecumenical vocation. This could happen because of L'Arche's orientation toward placing people who are labeled as intellectually disabled at the core of communal life. Welcoming and receiving the gifts of these persons, generally interested more in mutual relationships than doctrinal agreement, shapes community members in an ethos that makes encounter possible. Thérèse Vanier notes how an aspect of this comes from learning how to relate to the other nonverbally. Living at the pace of the slowest in communal life trains members in a nonviolent respect and approach to the body, where the nondisabled learn how to "bow down before the mystery of another human being and thus before the mystery of God."[16] In the midst of the inevitable conflicts of communal life, living from the two pillars of God's providence and relationship with the rejected helps to bring persons to that identity of truthfulness that unifies and builds up the body: "The nature of our communities and our determination to be an international

---

14. Vanier, *Our Journey Home*, 193.
15. Vanier, "Fragility of L'Arche," 30, 34-5; Vanier, *Befriending*, 38.
16. Vanier, *One Bread*, 80.

'family' incorporating a disconcerting diversity of individuals convinces me that the only thing uniting us is our common humanity."[17]

Jean Vanier understands L'Arche as called to the same (unintentional) role Francis of Assisi and his brothers discerned for their new community: to rebuild the church from the ground up. "We too have received a call to rebuild the Church and to work for unity between churches and between all people," he wrote. "We too have been sent forth on a mission today, with all our limits and fragilities, to announce the beauty and importance of people with disabilities, the importance of each person."[18] At the heart of this mission is a readiness to be befriended by and befriend the poor and marginalized as the key to renewal. In L'Arche, the secret to unity lies in relationships with the "strange/er," friendships that transform xenophobia into *philoxenia*, from hatred of the foreigner to love of the foreigner.

FOOTWASHING IN L'ARCHE: PRACTICING UNITY

L'Arche does not think itself into substantive moral community and Christian unity, but more importantly practices its way there. Engaging in communal practices forms persons and communities in the virtues and habits required to be a body open to a communion across a wide range of difference, and trains persons in the way of life commensurate with their ultimate aim. The practice I will focus on is the liturgical rite of footwashing as performed in L'Arche communities. Footwashing has existed within the church's worship since the early church, even if it has often been performed on the church's periphery.[19] Most traditions that have performed footwashing have interpreted the rite as one of humble service. While other minority themes have been recalled for the rite—such as cleansing, forgiveness, and following Jesus to the cross—the service theme has remained dominant. I see L'Arche's appropriation of the tradition as presenting the church with a renewed interpretation of the rite, which can potentially open a way for Christians to become a more unified body.

---

17. Ibid., 88.

18. Vanier, *Our Life Together*, 525.

19. A substantive treatment of footwashing in the Christian tradition has yet to be written. For clues, see Knight, "Feet Washing"; Richter, *Die Fusswaschung*; Beatrice, *La lavanda*; Thomas, *Footwashing*; Jeffrey, *A New Commandment*; Henn, "Emancipatory Inversion," chapters 2-4.

Living Traditions

L'ARCHE'S DISCOVERY OF FOOTWASHING

It is important to note that L'Arche did not immediately experience or understand footwashing as an important liturgical rite. As a movement founded in a 1960s French village, the Eucharist seemed the Christian practice most essential to L'Arche's existence. Yet as L'Arche grew beyond France, it encountered Christian communions other than the Roman Catholic Church. Not all of them placed the same emphasis on the Eucharist as a unifying sacrament. Take the founding of L'Arche in the UK as an example. Here the Roman Catholicism of Trosly, embodied in co-founder Thérèse Vanier, met the native Church of England. Much common ground was found between the two, but the debate over eucharistic intercommunion remained tense and sometimes even rancorous. Both sides wanted the Eucharist to be a sacrament of communion grounding the Body, but respecting the guidelines of the communion (the Roman Catholic in particular) meant no intercommunion.

In the midst of this impasse, another Christian communal practice was developing in UK L'Arche communities: the washing of feet on Maundy Thursday. Begun in some individual L'Arche homes, the rite eventually was practiced by whole communities. While I cannot locate an epicenter of the performance of footwashing in L'Arche, the rite now reaches from Canada, (where I have experienced it myself in various communities and L'Arche retreats) to India, France, and beyond. As Thérèse Vanier notes, in the midst of divisions and diverse practices, "The sacrament in which we can *fully* share, in which we can fully participate, is the washing of the feet."[20] "We are debarred from sharing the Eucharist," Helen Reid Thomas remarks, "but in washing one another's feet we are able to express both our unity and the mutuality of our relationships and over the years this liturgy has become a focal rite in our [UK] communities."[21]

BECOMING FRIENDS:
A NEW INTERPRETATION OF FOOTWASHING

The servant theme of footwashing, the dominant way it has been perceived in the Christian tradition, certainly presents itself in L'Arche. Yet I see L'Arche going deeper in its theological reflection of footwashing than merely

---

20. Vanier, *One Bread*, 56.
21. Thomas, *L'Arche Communities*, 53.

the affirmation of servant leadership—not that we no longer need to hear this! I contend that L'Arche goes further, by understanding footwashing as a rite which remembers Jesus offering us his friendship and calling his followers to bring that same invitation to the world, particularly to those most marginalized and oppressed. When communities faithfully perform Jesus' command, they can help facilitate a unity only the Holy Spirit can realize.

In his reflections on the practice of footwashing in the Gospel of John, as well as in L'Arche communities, Jean Vanier stresses the kenotic nature of Jesus' performance. Jesus does not simply become low to demonstrate his generosity, but does so to call his disciples friends. By removing his outer garments, Jesus abandons the status of superior and removes any obstacles to the intimacy of mutual friendship. According to Vanier, Jesus "presents himself to his disciples just as a person, a friend. Before being Lord and teacher, he is a heart, seeking to meet other hearts, a friend yearning to be in communion with friends, a loving person seeking to live in the heart of his friends."[22] Through letting their feet be washed, the disciples say "yes" to the gift of God's friendship, which shows how friendship is not merely made, but also received. For example, my guess is that Peter was as desirous of Jesus' friendship as anyone else in the upper room. Jesus meets his original denial of having his feet washed with a claim that this means Peter can have no participation with him. As Vanier paraphrases Jesus' response, "If I do not wash your feet, we are no longer friends. You can leave. Everything is over between us."[23] Vanier boldly takes Jesus' words about the mandatory nature of footwashing seriously by reiterating that it "is not a new ritual that we can follow or not or that we can accomplish at certain moments. It is an essential part of his message of love."[24] Jesus' followers obey his word by washing the feet of others, thus extending the invitation to friendship they were given and making it an aspect of the mission of the Christian community.

L'Arche's practice of footwashing can exemplify this friendship interpretation of the rite. Core member Philip Yates, from L'Arche Lambeth, speaks to footwashing as a sacrament of friendship when he notes his experience of washing the feet of nondisabled assistant Thierry. "*I washed Thierry's feet* . . . When I washed his feet I was thinking that I was his friend . . . I like washing the other person's feet most. When I do it for someone else I

---

22. Vanier, *Scandal of Service*, 19.
23. Vanier, *Befriending*, 42.
24. Vanier, *Drawn into the Mystery*, 229.

feel very clean. *I feel happy when we wash each other's feet because we do it to one another; we do it to be friends. It helps us to be together, to live together."*[25] Footwashing here is truly a divinely inspired sacramental event that not only demonstrates communion, but brings it about as well.

This kind of communion, however, does not merely include the individual person, but also builds the mutual relationships with other Christians needed for a unified community. As assistant Maggie Smith, from L'Arche Kent, notes, "Bending low before each other we wash each other's feet. It's precisely in those parts of me where I least accept myself that Jesus seems to want to meet me . . . He wants to meet me there so that I can become part of him, of his body. And in the community we seek to meet each other there so that together we can truly become a body that is holy."[26] Many persons in L'Arche experience footwashing as an event that enhances, bolsters, and unifies the body in the core virtues which make community happen: trust, humility, gentleness, and patience, to name just a few. In the midst of communal division and a plurality that can appear impossible to reconcile, persons in L'Arche have found footwashing to be a sacrament that unifies people in their common humanity and fellowship as children of God.

Perhaps this is why Vanier boldly brought the rite to a meeting of the Central Committee of the World Council of Churches. Asked to lead a retreat day on spirituality in the fall of 1997, Vanier invited the Committee to wash one another's feet as a sign of unity, humility, and forgiveness. Even Vanier was touched by the event, noting how "It was particularly moving to witness an Orthodox bishop kneeling down and washing the feet of an American woman who was a Baptist minister. Gestures sometimes speak louder and more lastingly than words. It was a moment of both grace and unity."[27] In the midst of a divided church, its leaders could take a moment to perform Jesus' command to be one as he and the Father are one. Vanier took what he learned about the power of washing feet from people like Philip Yates and offered it to the Central Committee as a sacrament of friendship and communion.

---

25. Wilson, *My Life Together*, 56.

26. Ibid., 53.

27. Vanier, *Drawn into the Mystery*, 230. See also Vanier, *Our Life Together*, 438, and Spink, *The Miracle*, 234-5.

CONCLUSION

What might happen if the rest of us, each ensconced in our own ecclesial communions, would do the same? How might our ecumenical efforts be renewed, aided, or transformed by making footwashing the rite we share in as Christ's followers? Might bowing down before one another as friends, bring us closer together and act as an evangelical witness to Christ's nonviolent redemption and reconciliation of the world?

I believe that L'Arche communities, even amidst their own imperfections and incompleteness, can lead the church in becoming more herself by offering a gentle and public faith to the late modern West. L'Arche demonstrates what a contemporary, substantive moral community might look like, based on an anthropology centered in relationships, rather than rights: a community where sacramental practices, rather than doctrinal agreements, represent the starting place for Christian unity.

Are there signs of unity in the church and world today that might convince cynics like me? Yes. Many of them live on the unassuming edges of our cultures, where persons labeled as disabled and nondisabled bend down to wash each other's feet, both daily and liturgically. By taking their lead, the church might both renew its own practices and grow into the mutual friends of Christ called to be one as Jesus and the Father are one.

BIBLIOGRAPHY

Beatrice, Pier Franco. *La lavanda dei piedi. Contributo alla storia della antiche liturgie cristiane.* Rome: CLV-Editione Liturgiche, 1983.

Gregory, Brad. *The Unintended Reformation: How a Religious Revolution Secularized Society.* Cambridge, MA: Belknap Harvard University Press, 2012.

Henn, Katherine Gabler. "Emancipatory Inversion and Ecclesial Identity: Text, Context and Ritual Interpretations of Johannine Footwashing." Ph.D. dissertation. Drew University, 2006.

Jeffrey, Peter. *A New Commandment: Toward a Renewed Rite for the Washing of Feet.* Collegeville, MN: Liturgical Press, 1992.

Knight, G. A. Frank. "Feet Washing." In *Encyclopaedia of Religion and Ethics*, vol.5, 814-23. Edited by James Hastings. Edinburgh: T&T Clark, 1912.

MacIntyre, Alasdair. *After Virtue: A Study in Moral Theory*, 3rd ed. London: Bristol Classic, 2007.

Richter, Georg. *Die Fusswaschung im Johannesevangelium: Geschichte ihrer Deutung.* Regensburg: Pustet, 1967.

Spink, Kathryn. *The Miracle, the Message, the Story: Jean Vanier and L'Arche.* Toronto: Novalis, 2006.

Living Traditions

Thomas, Helen Reid. *L'Arche Communities: Ecumenical Communities for People with Learning Disabilities*. London: Catholic Truth Society, 2002.

Thomas, John Christopher. *Footwashing in John 13 and the Johannine Community*, 2nd ed. Cleveland, TN: CPT Press, 2014.

Vanier, Jean. *An Ark for the Poor: The Story of L'Arche*. Ottawa: Novalis, 1995.

———. *Befriending the Stranger*. Grand Rapids: Eerdmans, 2005.

———. *Community and Growth*, rev. ed. New York: Paulist, 1989.

———. *Drawn into the Mystery of Jesus through the Gospel of John*. New York: Paulist, 2004.

———. "The Fragility of L'Arche and the Friendship of God." In *Living Gently in a Violent World: The Prophetic Witness of Weakness*, 30-35. Edited by Stanley Hauerwas and Jean Vanier. Downers Grove: IVP, 2008.

———. *Made for Happiness: Discovering the Meaning of Life with Aristotle*. Toronto: House of Anansi, 2001.

———. *Our Journey Home: Rediscovering a Common Humanity Beyond our Differences*. Ottawa: Novalis, 1997.

———. *Our Life Together: A Memoir in Letters*. Toronto: HarperCollins, 2007.

———. *The Scandal of Service: Jesus Washes our Feet*. Ottawa: Novalis, 1996.

Vanier, Thérèse. *One Bread, One Body: The Ecumenical Experience of L'Arche*. Ottawa: Novalis, 1997.

Wilson, Hilary. *My Life Together: L'Arche Communities and the Challenge of Unity*. London: Darton, Longman and Todd, 2004.

3

Ecclesia semper reformanda?
Reforming the Church Before, During, and After the Reformation

Sean A. Otto

2017 SIGNALED THE FIVE hundredth anniversary of an act that traditionally marks the start of the Reformation. In October 1517, Martin Luther, still a member of the Augustinian order, posted his 95 Theses on the door of the castle church in Wittenberg, desirous of participating in a scholastic disputation about indulgences. While Luther became more radical over his career, he never desired–as much as he criticized her teachings and morals–to break with the Church of Rome, and he, like every reformer before and after, certainly did not think of himself as starting a new church. A reformer is always seeking, after all, to restore the church to its pristine doctrine and life, in imitation of Jesus Christ and his apostles. This, of course, is no simple task. As I shall attempt to demonstrate in this chapter, it is one that has been continuous throughout the church's history and remains an important task for those who would "let the same mind be in you that was in Christ Jesus" (Phil 2:5).

One could argue that reforming the church goes back to the beginning of humankind, at least as it is portrayed in the Bible. Adam and Eve did not live very long in the Garden of Eden, before they turned against God's command not to eat the fruit of the tree of the knowledge of good and evil; they were ejected (Gen 3). The search for reconciliation with the creator has been ongoing ever since. The Israelites grumbled, complained, and were constantly brought back into correct relationship with God throughout the story related in the Torah, the historical books, and the Prophets. God's own Son—the Word Incarnate, God come to dwell among humans—dealt continually in his earthly ministry with the doubts, complaints, and sins of the people he had come to save through his atoning sacrifice on the cross. In the early church, there were signs of disunity and a need to return to God; examples include the apostles Peter and Paul in conflict (Gal 2); Peter dealing with those who wanted to maintain the kosher food laws as mandatory for both Jewish and Gentile Christians (Acts 10:1–11:18); or as in any number of incidents related in the Pauline epistles in which the apostle to the Gentiles sought to confirm, among the various churches he had founded around the Eastern Mediterranean, the Gospel he received from Christ Jesus.

Nor did the divine-human relationship improve after the apostolic period. A continual negotiation, of what might be deemed, a true and a continual search for a restoration of proper relationship continued. The list of early Christian heresies is impressive: Arianism; Adoptionism; Apollinarianism; Sabellianism; Nestorianism; Monophysitism; Monothelitism; Patripassionism; Pneumatomachianism; Docetism; Manichaeism; Priscillianism; Pelagianism; Semipelagianism; Montanism; Marcionism; Donatism; and for good measure, iconoclasm. Most of these positions resulted from a series of attempts to correctly understand and describe the nature of God as trinitarian, and to understand how God could become human in the second person of this Trinity. Arius taught, among other things, that the Son was created by the Father, and was named "Son" only as a title of courtesy. Docetism taught that the Word only *seemed* (from the Greek verb *dokeo*[set macron over o]—to seem) to become incarnate. Iconoclasm was about the nature of God, as *iconodules*, that is, those who venerate icons, argued that since the second person of the Trinity had taken on flesh, it was possible to portray the sacred in material form, keeping in mind, of course, that the icons themselves were not to be worshiped, but were to help those honoring them to worship God more fully and eagerly. This is quite a list of disagreements, many of which were already hotly debated in the second and third centuries, although the fourth century was probably the time of the greatest fervor.

How were these debates to be concluded? How was the church to be one, as the Son and the Father are one? The answer, of course, was to call a council and to discuss the issues amongst the most learned representatives of the church. There were a number of councils and synods that met to work out solutions to these disagreements, the most famous of them being: the Ecumenical Councils of Nicaea I and II (325, 787); Constantinople I, II and III (381, 553, 681); Ephesus I (431); and Chalcedon (451). These great councils were spread across four and a half centuries. They were called after the conversion of Emperor Constantine, which for convenience's sake we can date to shortly after the turn of the fourth century and the famous Battle of the Milvian Bridge (312). The early church historian, Eusebius of Caesarea, took Constantine's conversion as a watershed moment. While Eusebius might have been one of Constantine's greatest admirers, and sought to confirm the emperor's holiness and place in history, he was not entirely wrong in his estimation that the emperor's effect on the church was profound.[1] Increasingly from the time of the Edict of Milan (313), which legitimized Christianity without making it the official religion of the Empire, the role of the emperors in the life of the church changed. Whether this was for better or worse is much debated.[2] Whereas previously the Empire had persecuted Christians, it sought to protect and promote them, and to participate in the formulation of doctrine. It was, after all, Constantine who called the first Council of Nicaea.

Creedal statements emerged from the early councils. Today many churches use the creed developed by the First Council of Nicaea, later refined at the First Council of Constantinople, as well as: the Apostles' Creed, which is understood to be in accordance with the faith of Christ's closest and earliest followers; and the so-called Creed of St. Athanasius, also known as the *Quicunque vult*, which is still part of the official liturgy of the Anglican Church of Canada in the 1962 *Book of Common Prayer*. Although it has fallen out of fashion, especially since it has long been recognized not to have come from the pen of the sainted bishop of Alexandria, nonetheless, the *Quicunque vult* is a strong doctrinal statement without truly being a creed. It is a statement of belief, descriptive rather than affirmative, impersonal rather than personal. It does not begin, "I (or we) believe," but rather, "Whosoever desires to be saved, must above all things hold the Catholic Faith. Unless a man keeps it in its entirety inviolate, he will assuredly perish eternally."[3] There follows a strong series of statements about the

---

1. See Eusebius, *Ecclesiastical History*, and especially his *Life of Constantine*.
2. See Roth, *Constantine Revisited*.
3. Kelly, *Athanasian Creed*, 17.

triune nature of God and the nature of the Incarnation. This statement is scrupulous in its wording and enshrines an Augustinian theology of Trinity and Incarnation.[4] It seems to have been written with the heresies of Sabellius (modalism) and Arius (who denied the divinity of Christ) in mind, although J.N.D. Kelly points to its language not "as an engine for silencing heresy, but a constructive exposition of Catholic orthodoxy."[5] The interaction between the *Quicunque vult,* and the opinions it sought to correct, is precisely the sort of interaction I wish to highlight. Orthodoxy and heresy are negotiated terms. Reform, in this case, is an attempt to reform the popular Arianism of the late antique Iberian peninsula; it can be seen as a calling back to proper understanding and proper relationship. In this sense reform is positive: it is not simply stating that one opinion or another is incorrect. Rather, it is offering a "positive exposition" of what one believes is right, true, and good. Thus, the rise of creedal statements was in reaction to controversy in the early centuries of the church.

The situation of the church remained fluid throughout these centuries. As Christians began to adjust to their new place within the Roman Empire, after the conversion of Emperor Constantine, and the adoption of Christianity as the empire's official religion under Emperor Theodosius I, unprecedented threats to the Roman hegemony arose. There was an influx of various "barbarian" peoples into the territories ceded by the defeat and withdrawal of the legions, accompanied by a gradual collapse of centralized authority in the West. These events culminated in the sack of Rome in 410 (which shocked Augustine of Hippo considerably),[6] and the eventual removal of the emperor of the West in 476 by Odoacer, a descendent of

---

4. Ferguson, "Creeds, Councils, and Canons," 433: "Whereas earlier confessional statements had been more concerned with the doctrine expressed than with the wording itself, in the fifth and subsequent centuries there was an emphasis on scrupulous adhesion to exact wording. This was manifested in the West in the so-called Athanasian Creed (Quicunque vult), deriving from Spain or southern Gaul in the fifth or sixth century and enshrining the theology of Augustine, which required belief in its statements as necessary for salvation."

5. Kelly, *Athanasian* Creed, 76–7. He also writes in relation to the damnatory clauses: "[W]hen we study this section of the creed, we should remember that the ancient Church had a confident dogmatism which had little use for the scruples which trouble us. The sentiment, we should note, is inspired by Mk vi.16 ('he who believes and is baptized shall be saved, but he who does not believe shall be damned')." Nestorianism might also be a target. See ibid., 95–6.

6. See Augustine, *De civitate Dei*, and *On the City of God*, which was written in response to those who claimed the sack was punishment for abandoning the old gods (Augustine, *Retractationes* 2,43,2)

Edeco, one of Attila the Hun's most trusted lieutenants.[7] Then there was the explosive growth of Islam, which spread from Persia to Iberia in a century and a half, disrupting the entire Mediterranean world—both the world of Christianity and the world of the empire.[8] Councils and synods continued to be held to deal with controversies surrounding doctrine and practice, in both the East and the West, though increasingly East and West were isolated one from the other over issues of practice, such as: the use of leavened or unleavened bread in the Eucharist; whether priests should have beards; whether priests should marry. Relations deteriorated to the point of schism, mutual recrimination, and excommunication. The wound has yet to be fully healed, despite numerous attempts at reconciliation at various councils over the past ten centuries, signaling a continuous failure of reform, as it were.[9]

In the West, at least for a while, the issues turned more toward morals rather than doctrine, as the reforming papacy of the eleventh century sought to regulate the behavior of the clergy, to separate them from the laity, and to take tighter control of appointments to ecclesiastical office, which had been an area of contested authority between secular rulers and popes for some time in the so-called investiture controversy.[10] The behavior and suitability of the clergy continued to be an issue, one that would occupy leading churchmen throughout the Middle Ages and beyond. Holy Roman Emperor Henry V and Pope Calixtus II worked out a compromise over the issues of who controlled appointments to ecclesiastical office by the middle of the twelfth century, with the Concordat of Worms of 1122.

Further attempts at reform culminated in the famous Fourth Lateran Council of 1215, which issued legislation requiring all Christians to receive the Eucharist and to make confession to their priest once a year.[11] To help further these reforms, there were also efforts made at this, and subsequent councils, to raise the level of education amongst the clergy. Out of this same movement for reform grew the mendicant orders of St. Francis and

7. On this see Thompson, *Romans and Barbarians*.

8. An older view of the impact of Islam on Europe, and one now much contested, is that of Pirenne, *Mohammed and Charlemagne*. Cf. Brown, "'Mohammed and Charlemagne'" and Scott, *Mohammed and Charlemagne Revisited*.

9. A good overview of the relationship between East and West is, Chadwick, *East and West*. See also Congar, *After Nine Hundred Years*.

10. On these topics see Robinson, *The Papacy*, and Cushing, *Reform and Papacy*.

11. The decrees of Lateran IV and other councils are available in Tanner, *Decrees of the Ecumenical Councils*.

Living Traditions

St. Dominic, who focused on poverty, humility, and preaching—orthodox responses to the fervor that gave strength to the dualistic Cathars, and that brought forth the Waldensian movement, likewise focused on preaching, poverty, and humility.[12]

The challenge posed by Catharism brought doctrine to the forefront of controversy once again. Cathar dualism challenged some of the most fundamental teachings of the Catholic Church, for they posited a second creative principle; they utterly rejected the material world, which undermined a Catholic understanding of the Incarnation; and they rejected the church's sacraments in favor of their own. Yet there was always a strong moralistic element to these controversies, which is another common theme of reform. The appeal of the Cathar perfects (leaders) had much to do with their perceived moral purity, as they lived in poverty and chastity, virtues espoused but seldom met by the Catholic clergy. They also offered the average believer a sure means to salvation without the struggle with sin that was traditionally preached: first by explaining that the whole material world is evil and to be left behind through an upward progression of the divine spark through a series of incarnations; and second, by taking the burden of spiritual perfection upon themselves. Preaching missions, crusades, and inquisitions put down the Cathar threat and returned to the Catholic fold the sizable minority of Southern French and Northern Italians who had gone over to the dualists. Reform of the clergy's morals and of the practice of penance helped to consolidate these gains.

The growth of schools and universities in Europe, and the expanded study of the arts and theology, both helped to improve the education of the clergy, and introduced new fora in which theological speculation could lead to censure, as the limits of orthodoxy were tested again and again.[13] Calls for reform could emerge from these speculations, as they did with figures like William of Ockham, who sought to defend Franciscan poverty against the pragmatism of the popes, who in turn sought to keep the order within the bounds of the church.[14]

Among the more famous reformers of the medieval period, John Wyclif, emerged from the lecture halls of the University of Oxford in the

---

12. See Lambert, *Medieval Heresies*, 41–96.

13. See Fichtenau, *Heretics and Scholars*; Thijssen, *Censure and Heresy*; and Larsen, *School of Heretics*.

14. On Ockham's struggle with the papacy see Shogimen, *Ockham and Political Discourse*. On the Franciscan poverty controversy, see Lambert, *Franciscan Poverty*.

second half of the fourteenth century, venting his deep frustration in numerous treatises, polemical pieces, and sermons against the many abuses he perceived in the church's doctrine and practices. At heart, a pastor who cared deeply about the souls of the faithful, Wyclif took aim at the church's teaching on the Eucharist, penance, and clerical rights to own property and to receive obligatory tithes from the faithful. He questioned the moral authority of the popes who had allowed the church to grow rich and fat, while neglecting her obligations to believers.[15] Another schism in the papacy, precipitated by a double papal election in 1378,[16] along with strong support and protection from the exceedingly powerful John of Gaunt, meant that Wyclif was not condemned until long after his death. His reforming ideals took root in England. A popular movement, which came to be known, like so many other movements, by a pejorative term (Lollardy), kept them alive through the fifteenth and into the sixteenth century. These ideas never won general acceptance among either the clergy or the laity, and their effect on the Henrician Reformation is questionable.[17] Wyclif's call for reform might be characterized as the negative sense of reform. His anger at the abuses he perceived in the church's life and doctrine is palpable from his writings, especially his later works, and he decidedly and forcefully told the church what not to do, and told his opponents that they were wrong. All of Wyclif's venom should not blind us to the fact that he also offered a positive construction of what it is to be a Christian, one grounded firmly in the scriptures and in *imitatio Christi*, for Christ is the true measure of the faith.

The fifteenth century was marked by two very strong, but ultimately opposed movements for reform in Europe. On one hand was the Conciliarist movement that sought, by recourse, to the authority of a general council, to end the papal schism that had helped to stall the prosecution of Wyclif and had set off widespread anxiety about everyone's place within the Church Universal.[18] On the other hand was the reform movement, which took root in Bohemia and solidified around the person of Jan Hus and the issues of morality among the clergy, access to the chalice for the laity, and entwinement with Czech nationalism.[19]

---

15. The best introduction is Lahey, *John Wyclif.*
16. See Rollo-Koster and Izbicki, *Companion to the Great Western Schism.*
17. See Hornbeck, *Companion to Lollardy.*
18. On Conciliarism, see Oakley, *The Conciliarist Tradition.*
19. The classic study of Hussitism is Kaminsky, *History of the Hussite Revolution.*

Living Traditions

The two movements met head-on at the Council of Constance in 1415. The council had been called with the express purpose to end the schism, to deal with heresy, and to reform the church in head and members.[20] It was undoubtedly successful in the first of these purposes, as the council fathers managed to depose the three concurrent popes,[21] and to elect Martin V as sole and universally accepted pope. The success of the other two purposes is debatable, and it was here that the Bohemians and the Conciliarists ran into conflict. Jan Hus, a famous preacher and reformer in Prague, had been offered safe conduct to the council by Holy Roman Emperor Sigismund, but upon his arrival he was immediately thrown into prison and put on trial for heresy. He was convicted and burned at the stake on 7 July 1415. His death at Constance galvanized the reform movement in Bohemia, which went on to form an impressive military force under the leadership of "One-Eyed" Žižka, whose martial prowess held the forces of the Holy Roman Empire and the Roman Church at bay for twenty years. The armed conflict ended in compromise in the middle of the century, and if the council fathers thought that extending the chalice to the laity was heresy, then they certainly failed in its extirpation, since this was the main concession to the Bohemians.

The success of the third purpose of the Council of Constance, to reform the church, is even more questionable. The council did pass a pair of strongly conciliarist pieces of legislation, *Haec Sancta* and *Frequens*, the first of which asserted the ability of a general council to judge a pope, and the second of which decreed that a general council be called five and seven years after the Council of Constance, and then not more than every decade after that, since:

> The frequent holding of general councils is a pre-eminent means of cultivating the Lord's patrimony. It roots out the briars, thorns, and thistles of heresies, errors, and schisms, corrects deviations, reforms what is deformed, and produces a richly fertile crop for the Lord's vineyard. Neglect of councils, on the other hand, spreads and fosters the aforesaid evils. This conclusion is brought

---

20. On the reforms of the Council, see Stump, *Reforms*.

21. An earlier attempt at finding a conciliar solution to the schism at the Council of Pisa (1409) had led to the deposition of the Roman and Avignonese popes and the election of (antipope) Alexander V, who died within a few months and was replaced by (antipope) John XXIII. Neither the Roman nor Avignonese popes accepted their deposition, however, so the schism continued.

before our eyes by the memory of past times and reflection on the present situation.²²

To paraphrase: discussion of the faith in councils helps to call the faithful back to right belief and right relationship, but if the faithful do not meet together for discussion, then errors and schisms will grow, as can be plainly seen by reflection on the past and present difficulties of the church. This is a wonderful, optimistic proposition, and it seemed like it might work, since Pope Martin did call the immediate next councils. The optimism was short-lived, as struggle over who held authority—the council or the pope—began at the very next council. The papacy continued over the course of the century to consolidate its authority, to the detriment of conciliarist ecclesiology, which nonetheless continued "to compete stubbornly for the allegiance of Catholics with the high papalist or ultramontane vision of things."²³

Finally, we turn to the Reformation whose anniversary was marked in 2017. By now we have seen enough evidence to demonstrate that there were continuous attempts at reform by the time Martin Luther became disgruntled over the practice of indulgences in the early sixteenth century. Was Luther's reform different? I would argue that his was another in a long series of reforms, in some ways much more successful than previous efforts, and in some ways much less successful, but one focused on many of the same issues as previous efforts. People had problems with indulgences before Luther. John Wyclif and his followers had taken issue with them more than a hundred years earlier.²⁴ Likewise, theologians had been discussing how God's grace works in our lives since the very beginnings of the church. Of course, Luther knew this, for he, like all reformers, was searching for a return to the pristine, primitive church of Christ and the apostles. As to the Reformation's success or failure, it is certainly true that Luther fired the hearts of evangelical reformers all over Europe, and I think even the Roman Catholic Church would now acknowledge that much of his teaching was worthwhile and even correct. The Roman Church has agreed on a joint declaration on justification, for example.²⁵ I think the Reformation's

---

22. *Frequens*, in Tanner, *Decrees*, I:438–9; *Haec sancta* is found ibid., I:408–10.
23. Oakley, *Conciliarist Tradition*, viii. See esp. 20–59.
24. See Hudson, "Dangerous Fictions."
25. Lutheran World Federation and the Catholic Church, *Joint Declaration on the Doctrine of Justification*: http://www.vatican.va/roman_curia/pontifical_councils/chrstuni/documents/rc_pc_chrstuni_doc_31101999_cath-luth-joint-declaration_en.html [accessed 11 October 2017]

failures lie mostly in the repercussions of the fierce disagreements of the age. A nigh-total shattering of Christian unity in Europe and a series of internecine wars were devastating, and their effects long-lasting. These were never, of course, Luther's, or any other reformer's intention, for like his predecessors in reform, he sought to establish Christian truth and to reunite his brothers and sisters in Christ in a proper relationship with each other and with God. But in this, Luther's reform failed, and one could argue that it failed more fully than any previous attempt.

The history of the church following Luther's Reformation has been a history of churches. There were, of course, schisms before Luther's revolution, going back to the early Church and the non-Chalcedonian churches. The divides of the sixteenth and subsequent centuries are the ones that we feel most deeply in Europe and North America, and these are the divides that Western Christians have been trying to heal ever since. There have been glimpses of progress, like the *Joint Declaration on the Doctrine of Justification* mentioned above, and the near-reunion of Nonjurors and Greek Orthodox in the eighteenth century.[26] There have been many valiant attempts in the past century and a half to reach agreement on core doctrines, and to define what is essential to Christianity. The Chicago-Lambeth Quadrilateral of 1888 stands out as one example. It outlined the four essential qualifications for Christian reunification from an Anglican point of view: 1) the Holy Scriptures as rule of faith; 2) the Apostles' Creed as the baptismal creed and the Nicene Creed as sufficient expression of faith; 3) recognition of the two dominical sacraments; and 4) the historic episcopate, as variously adapted to local conditions.[27] The numerous meetings of groups such as the Anglican Roman Catholic International Commission, the creation of The United Church of Canada, and the communion between the Anglican Church of Canada and the Evangelical Lutheran Church of Canada are all other pertinent examples in this regard. Yet despite these efforts, well meaning and sincere as they are, Christians still do not, apart from a few exceptions, partake of the body and blood of Christ together, and this is the greatest scandal that has plagued Christians for centuries. How can Christians be one as Christ and the Father are one, if they cannot, or simply will not, eat the one bread which is Christ's body broken for them? If Christians

---

26. In the end, the Orthodox would not make an agreement because the Nonjurors were not the established ecclesial power in England. On Anglican-Orthodox dialogue, see Pinnington, *Anglicans and Orthodox*, and Elder, "Anglican-Orthodox Relations."

27. "Lambeth Quadrilateral," in Cross and Livingstone, *Oxford Dictionary*, 946. See also Draper, *Communion and Episcopacy*.

can find a way to share this bread and this cup, putting aside the differences of opinion as to what happens in that mystery, then perhaps they can have true communion.

Despite all these failed attempts to repair relationship, this should not leave us with a purely pessimistic view of reform in the church. The title of this chapter contains a question mark, and this was meant to highlight the ambiguity of the idea of *ecclesia semper reformanda*. Is it meant to be a factual statement or an aspirational statement? I think it is both. It is a factual statement as regards history: the history of the church, even the history of the world from a Christian perspective, can be seen as a search for a return to proper relationship and understanding, both with each other and with God; over time this has been more or less successful. It is an aspirational statement when we think about the present and our future: neither past failures, nor current failures, ought to give Christians any reason whatsoever to stop the effort of reform, or to stop the effort to bring ourselves back into proper relationship with ourselves, with our brothers and sisters, and with God. Further, the conciliar model, that is, a model based on dialogue, would seem on the face of it to be the most productive means of pursuing this, as history both ancient and modern demonstrates.

BIBLIOGRAPHY

Augustine of Hippo. *De civitate Dei*, 2 vols. Edited by B. Dombart and A. Kalb. Turnhout: Brepols, 1955.

———. *On the City of God Against the Pagans*. Edited and translated by R.W. Dyson. Cambridge: Cambridge University Press, 1998.

Brown, Peter. "'Mohammed and Charlemagne' by Henri Pirenne." *Daedalus* 103, no.1 (1974): 25–33.

Chadwick, Henry. *East and West The Making of a Rift in the Church: From Apostolic Times Until the Council of Florence*. Oxford: Oxford University Press, 2003.

Congar, Yves. *After Nine Hundred Years: The Background of the Schism Between the Eastern and Western Churches*. New York: Fordham University Press, 1959.

Cross, F.L. and E.A. Livingstone, eds. *The Oxford Dictionary of the Christian Church*, 3rd ed. Oxford: Oxford University Press, 2005.

Cushing, Kathleen G. *Reform and Papacy in the Eleventh Century: Spirituality and Social Change*. Manchester: Manchester University Press, 2005.

Draper, Jonathan. *Communion and Episcopacy: Essays to Mark the Centenary of the Chicago-Lambeth Quadrilateral*. Oxford: Ripon College Cuddesdon, 1988.

Elder, E. Rozanne. "Anglican-Orthodox Relations: A Long-Term Overview." In *One Lord, One Faith, One Baptism: Studies in Christian Ecclesiality and Ecumenism in Honor of J. Robert Wright*, edited by Marsh L. Dutton and Patrick Terrell Gray, 262-83. Grand Rapids, MI: Eerdmans, 2006.

Eusebius, *Ecclesiastical History*, 2 vols. Translated by Kirsopp Lake and J.E.L. Oulton. Cambridge, MA: Harvard University Press, 1926/1932.

Living Traditions

———. *Life of Constantine: Introduction, translation, and commentary*. Edited by Averil Cameron and Stuart G. Hill. Oxford: Oxford University Press, 1999.
Ferguson, Everett. "Creeds, Councils, and Canons." In *The Oxford Handbook to Early Christian Studies*, edited by Susan Ashbrook Harvey and David G. Hunter, 426-45. Oxford: Oxford University Press, 2008.
Fichtenau, Heinrich. *Heretics and Scholars in the High Middle Ages, 1000–1200*. Translated by Denise A. Kaiser. University Park, PA: Pennsylvania State University Press, 1998.
Hornbeck II, J. Patrick, with Mishtooni Bose and Fiona Somerset. *A Companion to Lollardy*. Leiden: Brill, 2016.
Hudson, Anne. "Dangerous Fictions: Indulgences in the Thought of Wyclif and His Followers." In *Promissory Notes on the Treasury of Merits: Indulgences in Late Medieval Europe*, edited by R. N. Swanson, 197-214. Leiden: Brill, 2006.
Kaminsky, Howard. *A History of the Hussite Revolution*. Berkeley: University of California Press, 1967.
Kelly, J. N. D. *The Athanasian Creed*. London: T&T Clark, 1964.
Lahey, Stephen E. *John Wyclif*. Oxford: Oxford University Press, 2009.
Lambert, Malcolm. *Franciscan Poverty: The Doctrine of Absolute Poverty of Christ and the Apostles in the Franciscan Order 1210–1323*, rev. ed. St. Bonaventure, NY: Franciscan Institute, 1998.
———. *Medieval Heresies: Popular Movements from the Gregorian Reform to the Reformation*, 3rd ed. Malden, MA: Blackwell, 2002.
Larsen, Andrew E. *The School of Heretics: Academic Condemnation at the University of Oxford, 1277–1409*. Leiden: Brill, 2011.
Lutheran World Federation and the Catholic Church. *Joint Declaration on the Doctrine of Justification*. http://www.vatican.va/roman_curia/pontifical_councils/chrstuni/documents/rc_pc_chrstuni_doc_31101999_cath-luth-joint-declaration_en.html
Oakley, Francis. *The Conciliarist Tradition: Constitutionalism in the Catholic Church, 1300–1870*. Oxford: Oxford University Press, 2003.
Pinnington, Judith. *Anglicans and Orthodox: Unity and Subversion, 1559–1725*. Leominster, UK: Gracewing, 2004.
Pirenne, Henry. *Mohammed and Charlemagne*. London: Routledge, 1958.
Robinson, I.S. *The Papacy 1073–1198: Continuity and Innovation*. Cambridge: Cambridge University Press, 1990.
Rollo-Koster, Joëlle and Thomas M. Izbicki, eds. *A Companion to the Great Western Schism*. Leiden: Brill, 2009.
Roth, John D., ed. *Constantine Revisited: Leithart, Yoder, and the Constantinian Debate*. Eugene, OR: Pickwick, 2013.
Scott, Emmet. *Mohammed and Charlemagne Revisited: The History of a Controversy*. Nashville, TN: New English Review, 2012.
Shogimen, Takashi. *Ockham and Political Discourse in the Late Middle Ages*. Cambridge: Cambridge University Press, 2007.
Stump, Philip H. *The Reforms of the Council of Constance (1414-1418)*. Leiden: Brill, 1994.
Tanner, Norman P., ed. *The Decrees of the Ecumenical Councils*, 2 vols. Washington, DC: Georgetown University Press, 1990.
Thijssen, J.M.M.H. *Censure and Heresy at the University of Paris, 1200–1400*. University Park, PA: Pennsylvania State University Press, 1998.
Thompson, E. A. *Romans and Barbarians: The Decline of the Western Empire*. Madison, WI: University of Wisconsin Press, 1982.

4

Most Modern of Churches?
Charles Taylor and the Baptist Inheritance
of the Reformation

Jesse Smith

THE WAKE CHURNED UP by Martin Luther's actions in 1517 continues to affect the ebb and flow of Western culture to this day. If a rising tide lifts all ships, the moment a fault line slips equally tosses them all at sea. The fault line slippage we now call the Reformation led directly to the intellectual climate of modernity. Christian interpreters of modernity, notably Louis Dupré and Charles Taylor, make cogent cases that the Reformation is among the most important historical events in the epochal change from the postclassical period to the modern era in the West.[1] This ecclesial revolution and its sectarian emanations produced various confessional "churches" that each instantiated particular cultural, geographic, linguistic, or dogmatic variations.

We know that the agents of reform often lost control of their own ideas. Movements produced doctrines that were abhorrent to the initial promulgators of reform. Luther abhorred the transmogrification of *sola fides* into a repudiation of paedobaptism. He also detested the iconoclasm of Zwingli. Calvin repudiated the elder Zwingli's assertion that the Eucharist was merely symbolic, even as he took up the mantle of reform in

---

1. Taylor, *Secular Age*; Dupré, *Passage*.

Switzerland. All these men found the Radical reformers, like Anabaptist Conrad Grebel, beyond the pale, even though a causal chain linked him to the mythical Wittenberg cathedral door.

All this to say that actions often have unintended consequences, and one of the dangers of a powerful idea is that it can escape the control of its initiator. Furthermore, when looking back at the diffusion of the ideal of the Reformation, it is tempting to read this history as a series of negative critiques. Once the harmony of European Roman Catholicism was shattered, discord and dissent inevitably followed. But such a reading of theological development denies the strong moral ideal enshrined in the task of reform and frames the relationship as one that is inherently antagonistic. Charles Taylor identifies this very error—the failure to understand the moral impetus— in relation to the modern spirit of individualism.[2] I will contend that the same high regard for individuals underpins the Baptist doctrine of soul liberty, and that they are cultural and theological equivalents. The congruence of both ideas extends to the similar aspersions and problems have dogged each.

Louis Dupré refers to the humanism of the renaissance and Reformation as the "passage to modernity," a necessary step in the evolution of the modern worldview.[3] Charles Taylor uses language of secularization in the development of a modern social imaginary over much of the same time frame. Bernard Lonergan emphasizes the *turn to the subject* as the key shift in modern philosophy and theology. The subject, the social imaginary, the value of humans qua humans: these combine in a world of individuals, a society that is less an interdependent web and more a collective in which each is uniquely valuable and separable. A picture emerges in this imaginary of the modern condition as one that is lived inside the mind before it is expressed in institutions. But institutions will inevitably emerge from the societies that are then in turn defined by them. What then, is a "modern" church? Alongside the claim that individualism emerges from moral ideals, there is both a connection between the experience of being a thinking, feeling person in the twenty-first century North Atlantic and an ecclesial expression, an institutional response to the theological *qualia* of what it is like to be a modern.[4] Insofar as modern individualism has a qualitative feel

---

2. Taylor, *Malaise*, 17.
3. Dupré, *Passage*, ix.
4. Nagel, "What Is It Like?"

that leads to corresponding institutional practices, Baptist institutions are among the most congruent.

BAPTIST ORIGINS

First a preliminary word of what I mean when I say *Baptist*. Without weighing in on the debate about the influence of early Anabaptists like the aforementioned Conrad Grebel, I will follow William Brackney and others who hold that Baptists trace their roots to 1609.[5] Attempts to renew religious life in England at the time were myriad, but can be divided into those who wanted to work within the framework of the Church of England and dissenters who took more radical positions. Many of these English dissidents campaigned for a separation of religious and civil power and took refuge in the Netherlands. There they began referring to themselves as Baptists. While they shared a belief in adult baptism with earlier Anabaptists, their respective plans for achieving recognition for their position were at odds. Men like Grebel and Menno Simons contended with civic authorities to assert their vision of ecclesiastic communities in a given region. When they lost, they sought new territories to instantiate their vision. That spirit continues to drive groups like the Hutterites, from Europe to the Canadian prairies and Pennsylvania, then on to Belize and Brazil. Baptist Dissenters, such as John Clarke and Roger Williams (founders of the colony of Rhode Island), did not share this need for homogeneity and instead argued for religious freedom.[6] Rather than sequester different confessions in particular regions, they contended that the human soul possesses the liberty to choose belief, uncoerced by civil or religious authorities. In fact, such free choice is a necessary condition to true faith. The term *soul liberty* and its cognate *soul competency* are first explicitly named in *The Axioms of Religion* by early twentieth-century Baptist theologian Edgar Young Mullins. Yet Brackney and Harmon identified the idea in Baptist writings from the seventeenth century.[7]

When the Apostle Paul declared that "for freedom Christ has set us free" (Gal 5:1), this was no idle statement. Luther himself points out that this liberty has nothing to do with civil liberty such as freedom from certain laws or taxes, nor is it what he calls carnal liberty, "by which people

---

5. Brackney, *Baptists*.
6. Barry, *Roger Williams*.
7. Harmon, *Baptist Identity*.

Living Traditions

obey neither the laws of God nor the laws of men, but do as they please."[8] He defines liberty as "liberty of conscience," in which the free Christian is sure of the support of God and of freedom from the wrath of God. As a sort of subtitle to his *De Libertate Christiana*, which is sometimes translated *A Treatise on Christian Liberty* (1520), Luther stated, "A Christian is a perfectly free lord of all, subject to none. A Christian is a perfectly dutiful servant of all, subject to all."[9] No longer *must* we obey earthly rules; we are bound only to act in love as dutiful children of God. That statement, which couples what we would call religious freedom and subsidiarity, marks a clear point at which Luther lost control of the force of his own ideas. Subsidiarity would go on to characterize Lutheran theology, while decentralized and unmediated freedom was the inheritance of the Radical Reformation.

CHARLES TAYLOR AND MODERNITY

In *The Malaise of Modernity*, Canadian Catholic philosopher Charles Taylor lists three inchoate worries that are accompanied by a sense of loss.[10] This formula (inarticulacy+worry+loss) is summed up by what he calls a malaise, and he identifies three that are felt by people living in the modern era. First is the malaise of individualism. It seems obvious that many or most in the West become detached from the grounding forces of filial piety, hierarchy, and duty, existing instead as atomistic moral agents, free to exercise our will. In Taylor's framework, we struggle to express a feeling that there must have been some halcyon era just beyond our memory when family and community bonds were deep and meaningful. What we feel has been lost is not just the bond, but also the very means to describe it. Second among the malaises is disenchantment. There is no longer a sacred structure investing the world with a surplus of meaning. Instead, things become *mere* things and all that remains is the appropriate categorization and distribution of said things. The final malaise concerns the loss of freedom. Without the mediating forces of family, tribe, or sacred order, the individual is practically helpless in the face of the hegemonic state. In *Malaise* and other works, Taylor tries to provide not only genealogies of these feelings, but also a grammar that will allow moderns to express themselves clearly.

---

8. Luther, *Commentary on Galatians*, emphasis added.
9. Luther and Svennung, *Martin Luther's Tractatus*.
10. Taylor, *Malaise*, 1–12.

Even a summation of those arguments is beyond the scope of this paper; what concerns us here is the first, the worry over individualism.

It is false to claim that individualism is a wholly modern invention, as if people could not understand their inner lives until the twentieth century. The interiority of Augustine's *Confessions* and the autobiographic style it spawned, as well as the skeptical self-analysis of Descartes clearly give us portraits of rich inner lives. But the type of individualism that emerges near the end of the eighteenth century is different in how the self emerges *sui generis*. As Dupré names the Renaissance the font of modern humanism, so Taylor describes the Romantic period as the font of modern authenticity. For Augustine, to look inward was to find God or at least the need for God, and then turn outward again. Thus the moral demands of life are found through introspection, but only insofar as we find in ourselves a connection to the outer cosmic order. For Rousseau and the Romantics who were responding to Enlightenment-style procedural reason, the inner self was a moral source in and of itself.[11] By attending to our sentiments, it was possible to adjudicate between good and evil. Something different is at work in this understanding of the moral life. This self-determination of morality, although connected to theistic explanations, is different from the Augustinian move in that it comes after the transformations wrought by procedural reasoning, as opposed to analogical or natural law archetypes. One does not find God inside oneself and then turn outward. The moral impulse is instead self-contained, and when one plumbs the depth of one's spirit, the result is not a circumflex gaze of the Divine, but the energizing impulse to live one's own moral life the best one can.

This is an unhinging of the internal sentiment from any external norming authority. While not directly addressed in either *Sources of the Self* or *Malaise of Modernity*, Taylor hints at what will become the main thrust of his argument in *A Secular Age*. The bedrock of all future secularities is in fact a change in the conditions of belief, and especially the mere possibility of unbelief.[12] So the cultural context of the shift of the conditions

---

11. Taylor, *Sources*, 355–70.

12. Taylor proposes a threefold vision of secularism, with each layer building on the last. Secularity (1) is the expulsion of religion from public life and the creation of an ostensibly neutral common social imaginary. Secularity (2) is the decline of religion, both belief and the practices engendered by these beliefs. Secularity (3) is "The conditions of experience of and search for the spiritual." The third is the oldest shift, and first is the version we most commonly associate with the term today. For a short treatment see Bellah, "Secularism." For a longer overview, which still pales before Taylor's 874 pages,

of belief is one that is explicitly Christian. But the context, after Rousseau, is no longer essential to the operation of the moral impulse. The moral impulse becomes acontextual, and indifferent to local conditions. Eventually, the discovery of an inner truth that must be enacted faithfully becomes a possibility even absent of Christian narrative. This is the need to live an authentic life.[13]

I might have created the impression that the malaises are wholly negative entailments of the atomization and disenchantment of the modern social order. For the "knockers" (Taylor's term) of modernity they are just that, the negative psychic damage caused by solipsistic individualism. The conservative (or more properly, revanchist) critique of modernity portrays the directionless and flattened social order, disenchantment, and powerlessness as just desserts for the prideful folly of individualism. Taylor's careful scholarship is not so quick to classify the malaises as some sort of retribution, as though humankind's decision to ignore the transcendent was willful folly that provoked the Divine *nemesis* of Greek tragedy.[14] Rather, there are positive claims and noble impulses to which the malaises can be only attributed *post facto*. The flattened social order is experienced as a malaise, and this feeling is provoked by the valorization of everyday life. Ideas of special status for any clerical or aristocratic order are still viewed with deep suspicion today, even though this entails the cultural instantiation of the principle "if everyone is special, then no one is special." In the second place, disenchantment is a consequence of decreased sacerdotalism and access to scripture in the vernacular. The positive goal of increasing access to the texts and practices of Christian faith has as an unintended consequence the disappointment of seeing what is behind the curtain (whether in the temple or in Oz). Finally, the powerlessness of atomized individuals is a consequence of the positive goal of personal responsibilisation. Responsibilisation is the process by which individuals personally become aware

---

see Smith, *How (Not) to Be Secular*.

13. A separate tradition of Christian authenticity is a major theme in the thought of Søren Kierkegaard. Perhaps because of the animosity Kierkegaard showed towards the thought of Hegel, and Taylor's own position as a committed Hegelian, the Dane's ideas do not feature prominently in Taylor's account of authenticity.

14. The structure of Greek tragedy is rooted in the idea that humanity (and therefore individuals) have a particular place in the world. Tragic figures like Oedipus were compelled by a particular type of pride (*hubris*) which, contrary to modern versions of pride as selfishness, was a failure to respect the natural order. Any act that transgressed a person's place in the world (*atë*) would be met by the judgement of the gods (*nemesis*) whose punishment was meant to keep the natural order in check.

of and then take responsibility for their moral reasoning. As Taylor sees it, when individuals bear greater responsibility for their moral status and eternal soul (rather than relying on the intercessory efforts of a clerical class or their embedded position within a kinship community) they are liable to feel paralyzed by the enormity of the task. Thus, the call to live an authentic life becomes both energizing and paralyzing.

With these two frames, we can begin to make connections. The individual with unmediated access to God (through the priesthood of all believers) and to the substance of the Christian faith (through unmediated access to the Bible) is a recipe for an individual equipped with all the necessary tools to create a religious life. In fact, in modernity the most authentic version of personal piety is the one we craft for ourselves. This path is carved with the continual awareness that for others, the particularities of that impulse may differ. This then requires two fundamental positions for any body of believers wishing to live authentic lives such as this. First is the intramural recognition that each and every Christian holds ultimate responsibility for their relationship with God. Adherence to confessions or similar litmus tests is denied as a sufficient basis for religious commitment (though this does not deny that such adherence could not generate genuine faith; it claims only that nothing is guaranteed). This is soul liberty at work.

Secondly, for authentic faith a civil environment must exist that allows for such a possible plurality of views. The archetypal declaration of this ideal is the establishment clause of the United States Constitution. Borrowed from the founding charter of Rhode Island, what is anachronistically referred to as the separation of Church and State is actually a space for belief to grow uncoerced, not an insistence that religion be kept out of politics *tout court*.[15] The clause, along with what is known as the Free Association clause, form the first amendment of the Bill of Rights, adopted in 1791. It reads in full: "Congress shall make no law respecting an establishment of religion, or prohibiting the free exercise thereof; or abridging the freedom of speech, or of the press; or the right of the people peaceably to assemble, and to petition the Government for a redress of grievances." The prohibition prevents "an" establishment (particular), not "the" establishment (general) of an ecclesial body, and it ensures no strictures are placed on the exercise.

---

15. The aim of the Establishment clause is to prevent the formation of a state-sanctioned church, such as the Church of England, which linked ecclesiastical authority to civic authority. The cliché "separation of Church and State" actually comes from a letter written by Thomas Jefferson to a Baptist congregation in Danbury, CT. See Jefferson, "Jefferson's Letter."

Since *establishment* and *free exercise* are not tautological, it is assumed that for the population to be truly free, no state-established church ought to set the terms of religious life.

The Baptist vision is one of religious liberty as necessary for spiritual growth. The ideal of liberty was transmitted through English dissidents to Europe's lowlands and the American Continent, where it significantly shaped the relationship between state and church. That influence was then re-transmitted back to Europe and magnified in the Republican ideals codified in the establishment of the first French Republic in 1792 (one year after the Bill of Rights was adopted and just over three years after the storming of the Bastille). As interlocked religious and secular powers were torn asunder in this and other conflicts, the supposed obviousness of state church allegiance was questioned. Following emotivist and expressivists turns during the Romantic Period, the moral instinct of individuals assumed a higher priority than at any previous point in history.[16]

Today, we are left with a cultural paradigm that enshrines the quality of authenticity as one of the most important factors in determining what human flourishing looks like. Accordingly, there is a way for each person to live life to the fullest, and the individual is the ultimate arbiter of just what that life ought to resemble. In soul liberty, we encounter the idea that this is a feature of the religious life in particular. There are also negative effects caused by the close alignment of Baptist dogma and modern accounts of identity. Baptists have few universal identifying features, but theologically they are united by promoting a minimalist two sacraments, baptism and communion. Because of its de-emphasis of liturgical practice, it would be extremely difficult to find a Baptist service ever described as being one of "smells and bells." Traces of Zwinglian ideas about worship and Eucharist as mere remembrance flatten the religious experience of worshippers –the theological equivalent of disenchantment.

Baptist congregations appeared at the juncture of British dissidence and Europe's radical reformation. In their efforts to create the religious communities they desired, without being forced to seek out lands not under the purview of a state church, they developed theological grounds for religious pluralism. This pluralism provided the social space for individuals to cultivate their own faith and gave those individuals the ultimate responsibility for their own spiritual status. We have now seen how this action, with its positive ideals (and unexpected negative effects) functions as an

---

16. Taylor, *Sources*, 368.

ecclesial correlation to Taylor's authentic self. In both the malaises that affect modern people and the desires that drive them, there are echoes of soul liberty's paralyzing responsibility and deep concern for the individual. While not claiming that it represents a more perfect expression of what life and believers ought to look like, this chapter should make clear that the possibility of—and conditions for—authenticity and Baptist polity flow from the same font.

BIBLIOGRAPHY

Barry, John M. *Roger Williams and the Creation of the American Soul: Church, State, and the Birth of Liberty*. New York, NY: Penguin, 2012.

Bellah, Robert N. "Secularism of a New Kind." The Immanent Frame (19 October 2007). https://tif.ssrc.org/2007/10/19/secularism-of-a-new-kind/

Brackney, William H. *Baptists in North America: An Historical Perspective*. Religious Life in America. Malden, MA and Oxford: Blackwell, 2006.

Bradbury, John P. "Non-Conformist Conscience? Individual Conscience and the Authority of the Church from John Calvin to the Present." *Ecclesiology* 10 (2014): 35-52.

Dupré, Louis. *Passage to Modernity: An Essay in the Hermeneutics of Nature and Culture*. New Haven: Yale University Press, 1993.

Harmon, Steven R. *Baptist Identity and the Ecumenical Future Story, Tradition, and the Recovery of Community*. Waco: Baylor University Press, 2016.

Jefferson, Thomas. "Jefferson's Letter to the Danbury Baptists [1 Jan 1802]." *Library of Congress Information Bulletin* 57, no.6 (June 1998). https://www.loc.gov/loc/lcib/9806/danpre.html.

Luther, Martin. *A Commentary on St. Paul's Epistle to the Galatians*. Translated by Erasmus Middleton. London: James Clarke & Co., 1953.

Luther, M. and J. Svennung. *Martin Luther's Tractatus de Libertate Christiana 1520*. Kleine Texte Für Vorlesungen Und Übungen. De Gruyter & Company, 1948.

Nagel, Thomas. "What Is It Like to Be a Bat?" *The Philosophical Review* 83, no. 4 (1974): 435–50.

Smith, James. *How (Not) to Be Secular: Reading Charles Taylor*. Grand Rapids, MI: Eerdmans, 2014.

Taylor, Charles. *A Secular Age*. Cambridge, MA.: Belknap Press of Harvard University Press, 2007.

———. *Sources of the Self: The Making of the Modern Identity*. Cambridge, MA: Harvard University Press, 1989.

———. *The Malaise of Modernity*. Concord, ON: Anansi, 2003.

5

Living Traditions, A Lutheran Perspective

Semper Reformanda of *Sola Scriptura, Sola Fide, Sola Gratia*

Kimberlynn McNabb

The publication of a new translation of the Book of Concord has been made desirable, if not necessary, by a number of considerations. In the first place, in so far as every translation is an interpretation, the tremendous advances must be taken into account which have been made during the last generation in our understanding of the literary and historical backgrounds of the documents included in this book. In the second place, allowance must be made for the literary tastes of modern readers for whom the English style of earlier generations seems heavy, cumbersome, and sometimes almost unintelligible. In the third place, the needs of those who may use the volume must be considered by furnishing them with quick and easy reference . . . and other tools essential to understanding and study.[1]

THIS EXCERPT IS FROM the 1959 edition of *The Book of Concord*. It is perhaps a strange place to begin. However, these founding writings are integral to Lutheran identity and Lutheran living in a changing world. The intent of this chapter is to suggest that Lutheranism is not the church of Martin

1. Tappert, *Book of Concord*, v.

Luther, and yet it continues to draw life from founding documents that have shaped the "theological Aesth-ethic" of the church (see below for a definition of this term). The chapter does not present new ideas, but rather highlights moments and thoughts of Living Word that express the continued work of reformation as applied to the Lutheran World Federation's "Reformation 500" theme. The style is a personal theological reflection from one who, although being baptized in a Presbyterian church, has been an active part of the Lutheran community since the age of five. Although of German decent, my formative experiences have included participation with Finnish, Danish, and Swedish congregations. My perspective is also shaped through study at Waterloo Lutheran Seminary (now Martin Luther University College) at Wilfrid Laurier University.

Growing up in a confessional church has meant living a hermeneutic of theological reflection informed by founding principles. This hermeneutic can be described as a "theological Aesth-ethic" that acts as a guiding principle for continued reformation. What does this mean? Consider that aesthetics is a hermeneutic that interprets information from the interaction with external objects where the senses, experience, and imagination combine with one's feelings to evaluate the world (beyond simply a philosophy of beauty, art, and taste). Combine this word with ethics, defined as a philosophy, both moral and spiritual in nature, that governs a person or a group's behavior, conduct, and way of being. Theological Aesth-ethic, then, is the hermeneutic that has continued to foster *semper reformanda* within Lutheran tradition ("always reforming"). This hermeneutic's foundation is grounded in the confessional theme of justification by grace through faith, or as one theologian describes, "For Luther, 'justification' refers to God's conversion of the human project. God in Christ enters human history, and we know that things will never be the same again."[2]

Lutherans continue to learn the Reformation slogans that for generations were the principles that influenced people within the tradition: *sola gratia, sola scriptura, sola fide*. This theological Aesth-ethic determined matters of church, faith, and life. This theological Aesth-ethic is a shared view, today held by a communion of 74 million people, representing 145 Lutheran church bodies in 98 countries around the world.[3] Lutheran Aesth-ethics is an articulation of an understanding of grace, hinged on the theology of the cross. It is mission and meaning, where the purpose

---

2. Jorgenson, *Awe and Expectation*, 16.
3. http://www.lutheranworldfederation.org/content/about_lwf

Living Traditions

is connecting ineffable beauty and profound tragedy, offering hope and a possibility of renewed relationships.[4] The Lutheran World Federation (LWF) has set a renewed theological Aesth-ethic to challenge the church to continue reformation, wrestling with the theme juxtaposed to present sensibilities. The theme (specifically chosen for the five hundredth commemoration[5] of the Reformation) is worded in this way: *Liberated by God's Grace—salvation, human beings, creation—not for sale*. This three-part theme is the theological Aesth-ethic and lens through which Lutherans are a living tradition within the world today, and answering the question so often repeated in *Luther's Small Catechism*, "What does this mean for us?" *Liberated by God's grace* is the current expression of the Reformation, and is part of a continued theological reform of language to speak to the times and proclaim grace. As a living tradition, Lutherans around the world have responded to the LWF's theme.

What these terms signify for us (*sola gratia, sola scriptura, sola fide*) took on new meaning and provoked renewed theological reflection during and after World War II. Just as *The Book of Concord* changed, language changed, so as to take into account tremendous horrors; to move from heavy and cumbersome (dead) theological words; and to reform the church toward intelligible and life-giving confessional living. World War II was a reminder of the truth in the confession of the liturgy:

> we are in bondage to sin and cannot free ourselves. We have sinned against God in thought word and deed, by what we have done and by what we have left undone. We have not loved you with our whole heart and we have not loved our neighbors as ourselves.[6]

World War II changed the conversations within Lutheran congregations, produced new generations of theologians and ethicists, and saw a highlighting of vocation and the priesthood of all believers.[7]

---

4. Brown, *Religious Aesthetics*, 185.

5. Note the intentional use of "commemoration," rather than "anniversary." For generations, Lutherans have held "rah-rah" Reformation services and celebrations near Oct. 31st of each year. Segments of the church have chosen to use "commemoration" as a way of remembering and respecting Reformation, but also recognizing that the Reformation led to violence, war, and persecution (at the hands of Lutherans to those deemed "other.")

6. ELCA, *Evangelical Worship*, 94.

7. Bloomquist and Stumme, *Promise*, 4.

Prior to and after World War II, Lutheranism as a way of life has been taught, as mentioned a moment ago, by *Luther's Small Catechism*. The section devoted to the Ten Commandments, the catechetical response to the question, "what does this mean for us?" begins with the words, "We are to fear and love God, so that we . . ." In this marking of five hundred years of Reformation, *we are to fear and love God, so that we,* through our lives, proclaim that "human beings are not for sale." As Bonhoeffer wrote:

> it is only by living completely in this world that one learns to have faith . . . By this-worldliness I mean living unreservedly in life's duties, problems, successes and failures, experience and perplexities. In so doing we throw ourselves completely into the arms of God, taking seriously not our own sufferings, but those of God in the world—watching with Christ in Gethsemane. That, I think, is faith; that is *metanoia*; and that is how one becomes a [human being] and a Christian.[8]

Remembrance Day 2007 fell on a Sunday. Lutherans who gathered for worship in Halifax, Nova Scotia were very much aware that the community gathered as a unique set of people representing "DPs" (displaced persons from places like Germany, Russia, Estonia, Latvia, and Prussia), along with former members of the Hitler Youth organization, families whose parents were Nazi soldiers, Canadian veterans, and present day military personal. Alongside them were Finns, Danes, and Norwegians who lived through the war in Europe or served abroad in their own military forces; newly arrived Germans; lifelong Canadians (some with German last names who recall family stories of abuse during the Great Wars); and newer refugees from war-torn areas in Kosovo and Ethiopia. One faith, one baptism, and a shared confession allowed this diversity to address the perplexities of being a community of faith. Bonhoeffer's words proclaim that fully entering life in the world means walking through the death of Christ. By doing so, one becomes a human being, filled with such grace that all are viewed as Christ's address to us. The address is an invitation demanding a response.

Living Word spoke through the mess of emotion and experience of Lutherans after World War II. Grace compelled an address to such chaos. In Canada, the address was the formation of Canada Lutheran World Relief, founded in 1946 in response to refugee and relief needs of postwar Germany.[9] The organization is a living tradition that supports efforts of

---

8. Bonhoeffer, *Letters and Papers,* 369-70.
9. http://www.clwr.org/who/history

the LWF, such as operating some of the largest refugee camps in the world. But this is not enough. Human beings are not for sale, as expressed in the Reformation Challenge of the Evangelical Lutheran Church in Canada (ELCIC). This challenge set a goal of bringing 500 refugees to Canada over the Reformation commemoration period. As of summer 2018, 540 refugees had been resettled.[10] It is one way that Lutherans live grace, proclaiming that human beings are not for sale.

We are to fear and love God, so that we, through our lives, proclaim that creation is not for sale. In the 1950s, Joseph Sittler wrote, "ecology, that is, the actuality of the relational as constitutive of all that lives, is the only theater vast enough for a modern playing out of the doctrine of grace."[11] This theological Aesth-ethic is evident in the biennial reports of the ELCIC and its Synods, particularly those of the past decade. For example, at the 2016 Eastern Synod Assembly, "delegates affirmed—in a vote of 96%-that church investment should reflect the values we hold as Christians. Afterwards, they heard a presentation outlining ELFEC's plan to put companies engaged in traditional oil-and-gas activities on the 'screen out' list for investment."[12] ELFEC, the Evangelical Lutheran Foundation of Eastern Canada, holds the invested monies of the church, and focuses on responsible investment, including environmental stewardship and impact investing (commonly green energy and technology), again living out a theological Aesth-ethic where creation is not for sale. Lutherans affirm that human beings are not for sale as they focus on human rights, labor rights, governance, economic/social justice, and global peace.[13]

For over a decade, the ELCIC has promoted Stewardship of Creation awards for those churches that are environmentally engaged through the retrofit of their buildings and incorporation of environmental projects. The ELCIC's Reformation Challenge included Lutherans' relationship with the environment. As a living tradition, congregations and individuals were encouraged to plant trees. As of 2018, 80,501 trees have been planted, with a goal of 500,000.[14] Consider how Sittler continued to express these convictions:

---

10. http://www.elcic.ca/ReformationChallenge/default.cfm
11. Sittler, *Evocations*, 85.
12. http://www.elfec.ca/sites/default/files/resources/elfec_report_2016_final.pdf., 10.
13. http://www.elfec.ca/invest-us
14. http://www.elcic.ca/ReformationChallenge/default.cfm

if grace is understood ecologically as built into the whole constitution of the world of nature, society, and the life of [humans] with fellow [humans], if grace is explicated from the standpoint of the doctrine of creation as bringing forth life-giving variety, then a quite new way of beholding the world and our fellow [human] comes into possibility. I then affirm not that I bestow grace or I invest with grace but that grace comes in black and white and yellow and red! Grace comes in colors. That is a quite different understanding of grace, for it is bound up with the unthinkable variety of God the Creator who loves all colors, textures, forms, nuances, and modes of life. It is grace as the joyful acknowledgement of the variety that God loves, the variety [God] has made. This is quite a different theological understanding from the moral conclusion that simply commands you to obey the commands of God.[15]

Lutherans live grace by proclaiming that creation is not for sale.

We are to fear and love God, so that we, through our lives, proclaim that "salvation is not for sale." Allen Jorgenson, a professor at Martin Luther University College, wrote:

> The theme of justification...underscore[s] the idea that God in Christ inverts the human project. We, who are by nature self-centered and prone to use others and the environment for our pet projects, have been put to death and made alive again. The new human is seen by God to reflect and bear the image of Christ, and is for that reason a recipient of the Holy Spirit, who renews us both from the inside out and from the outside in. This work of God has the salutary effect of making us stewards in the reign of God.[16]

Humans are stewards in the reign of God, not purveyors of salvation. The theme of "salvation not for sale," and the way salvation is presented to the world from a Lutheran theological Aesth-ethic, entail the inclusion of human beings as vessels of grace.

One such example is Bishop Munib Younan, bishop of the Evangelical Lutheran Church of Jordan and the Holy Land. He eloquently speaks of what it means to be a living tradition that lives out of a Lutheran theological Aesth-ethic. The church Younan serves is a church of 3000 Lutherans living in a Palestinian context, calling God "Allah," and living in relationship with Muslims for centuries. Lutherans in the region are known for mediation and peace building, peace education in their schools (which are multifaith,

---

15. Sittler, *Evocations*, 85-6.
16. Jorgenson, *Awe and Expectation*, 17.

Living Traditions

including a high percentage of Muslim students), and operating a women's desk addressing women's justice issues.[17] The church holds hope that through education they might be guarantors of building a modern society that includes religious and gender justice.[18] After decades of mass exodus by Christians, Younan continues to advocate for a Christian ministry of presence and accompaniment. To his thinking, if the church schools close, mission ends in the territory and there is no mediator between Muslims and Jews. In his keynote address to the Eastern Synod of the ELCIC in Toronto in June 2016, Younan noted that if we do not do it as Lutherans, no one will in this part of the Middle East. What does this mean? It means accompaniment where no church is so small that it cannot give, and no church is so big it cannot receive. Younan tells the church that not being ashamed of our faith is the best way to fight extremism.[19] Being vessels of grace is one way that Lutherans are a living tradition and proclaiming that salvation is not for sale.

Within Lutheran tradition, Reformation is an ongoing practice where contextual circumstances, or chaos on the global scale, prompt Lutherans to focus on renewed confessional living. Through five centuries, Lutherans have fallen short and have not lived as catholic, evangelical, and reforming Christians. Lutherans have not been good stewards of the means of grace and have taken a circuitous journey through and around *sola scriptura, sola gratia, sola fide*. This said, this chapter is a moment to emphasize Living Word and Good News as a tradition looks to the future. Since the time of Luther, each generation's expression of grace has been an expression of Living Word and living tradition. One finds this witness in a host of post-World War II theologians: Rudolph Bultmann, Paul Tillich, Helmut Thielicke, Edmund Schlink, Krister Stendahl, George Lindbeck, Martin Marty, Jaroslav Pelikan, Eric Gritsch, Robert Jenson, Carl Braaten, John Stumme, Karen Bloomquist, Nadia Bolz-Weber, and so on. With slightly different styles and to varied audiences, their theological Aesth-ethic was held in common. Rooted in confessional statements, each theologian used language common to their people to articulate grace and the proclamation of that grace: Living Word for a hurting world.

---

17. http://www.elcic.ca/ReformationChallenge/Scholarships.cfm

18. To date, the ELCIC as part of their Reformation Challenge has provided 166 scholarships to the Evangelical Lutheran Church of Jordan and the Holy Land.

19. Bishop Younan's speeches to the Assembly are available at http://www.eastern-synod.org/search/node/2016%20assembly

The heart of the Augsburg Confession and *The Book of Concord* is that Lutheran living centers on the biblical affirmation as expressed in Article IV:

> it is also taught among us that we cannot obtain forgiveness of sin and righteousness before God by our own merits, works, or satisfactions, but that we receive forgiveness of sin and become righteous before God by grace, for Christ's sake, through faith, when we believe that Christ suffered for us and that for his sake our sin is forgiven and righteousness and eternal life are given to us.[20]

Every re-creation of Article IV is "the essence of 'Living Word,' where God addresses the whole human race and unconditionally affirms them, freely giving the gift of grace."[21] The 2017 Lutheran commemoration of the Reformation has given Lutherans pause to once again re-articulate theological Aesth-ethic for present-day hearers. It is a time when the proclamation of Good News is spoken and lived through a translation of grace as "salvation, human beings, and creation, not for sale!" *Semper reformanda* is Living Word that is embodied as a theological Aesth-ethic and a calling where people and church proclaim in thought, word, and deed that we are liberated by God's grace "for the healing of the world."[22]

BIBLIOGRAPHY

Bloomquist, Karen, and John Stumme, eds. *The Promise of Lutheran Ethics*. Minneapolis: Augsburg Fortress, 1998.

Bonhoeffer, Dietrich. *Letters and Papers from Prison*. Edited by Eberhard Bethge. New York: Collier Books/Macmillan, 1953/1971.

Brown, Frank Burch. *Religious Aesthetics*. Princeton: Princeton University Press, 1989.

Canadian Lutheran World Relief. n.d. www.clwr.org/who/history.

ELCA (Evangelical Lutheran Church in America). *Evangelical Lutheran Worship*. Minneapolis: Augsburg Fortress, 2006.

Erlander, Daniel. *Baptized We Live: Lutheranism as a Way of Life*. Chelan, WA: Holden Village, 1981.

Evangelical Lutheran Church in Canada. n.d. www.elcic.ca/ReformationChallenge/default.cfm.

Evangelical Lutheran Foundation of Eastern Canada. n.d. www.elfec.ca.

Jorgenson, Allen G. *Awe and Expectation: On Being Good Stewards of the Gospel*. Eugene, OR: Wipf and Stock, 2010.

---

20. Tappert, *Book of Concord* 30.

21. Erlander, *Baptized*, 19.

22. Title of LWF Tenth Assembly 2003, Winnipeg.

Living Traditions

Lutheran World Federation. n.d. www.lutheranworldfederation.org/content/about-lwf.
Sittler, Joseph. *Evocations of Grace: Writings on Ecology, Theology, and Ethics.* Edited by Steven Bouma-Prediger and Peter Bakken. Grand Rapids: Eerdmans, 2000.
Tappert, ed. *The Book of Concord.* Philadelphia: Fortress, 1959.

6

There's Something About Mary
How a New Protestant Mariology Can Benefit Ecumenical Dialogue
Adrienne Findley-Jones

THE SUBJECT OF THE Blessed Virgin Mary is inevitably discussed between Protestants and Roman Catholics in ecumenical dialogue. While it has been traditionally seen as difficult, if not impossible at times, Protestants can indeed benefit more from including Mary into their spiritual practices than from their prolonged exclusion and reluctance. Like many of the reformers of his generation, Martin Luther remained devoted to her in his own practices. Yet there has been a great reluctance on the part of Protestants to embrace her as more than one amongst the cloud of witnesses and saints. While not elevating her to a status that would be difficult to reconcile within Protestantism, I am suggesting that a shift in focus is vital and necessary for Protestant-Roman Catholic and Protestant-Protestant dialogue to move past the traditional Marian stumbling blocks. There is something about Mary that is of importance to these traditions, and the language used to describe her as both the *Theotokos* and as the human being who sang the *Magnificat* has been one of the greatest complications in the dialogue. To neutralize the complication of language, a discussion of the difficulties of denominational identity, the interpretation of Mary herself, and where they intersect is important.

Living Traditions

Given the sheer number of Protestant denominations, generalizing Marian views in Protestantism is difficult. This paper will discuss elements of Anglican and Lutheran Mariologies as may best benefit the dialogue for potential interactions and areas for further study. Generally speaking, Anglicanism and Lutheranism are direct breakaways from the Roman Catholic Church in the sixteenth century. Thus it would be appropriate to see how they evolved in thought and approach to Marian teachings, and how those teachings come into conflict with Roman Catholicism. It also allows for a study into the potentially grey ecumenical area of denominational identity, as well as the presumed identity of the other partner. This will highlight a nuance of Mariology: how we have presumed and assumed Mary's own identity over the years, and how those presumptions have inhibited dialogue as partners became entrenched in their positions. As most of the ecumenical dialogue between Roman Catholics and Protestants has focused on the episcopacy and areas of ministry, the power of Mary's "yes" and her song of social justice can bring additional insight and means of creative missiology to the dialogue. It can be effective in dialogue with Protestants without the fear of compromising issues for Protestant identity or insulting the progress of interdenominational dialogue.

PROTESTANT MARIOLOGY: AN OVERVIEW

Mentioning Protestants and devotion to the saints in the same sentence is almost an oxymoron. Mary does not play a large role in the life of Protestant faith outside the biblical passages where she is mentioned by name or by reference. Yet her position is difficult to generalize due to the varied influences of Luther, Calvin, and other Reformers. While the Protestant Reformers of the sixteenth century all valued Marian piety, in more recent years, especially within the last hundred, Protestant views of Mary have changed. Instead of being the traditionally passive receptacle for the Christ child, "as a model of both motherhood and of female asceticism,"[1] she is now seen as a feisty and radical example for Christian women.[2] Thanks in part to interpretation of the *Magnificat*, she is now portrayed as being an example of social justice awareness, raising awareness of the injustices that would have plagued her and others like her through the centuries and today.

1. Kreitzer, "Luther Regarding," 250.
2. McKnight, "The Mary We Never Knew," 26, 28.

Roman Catholic forms of Marian piety and Mariology over the centuries are obstacles for Protestants.[3] The idea of Mary as "Mother of the Church" tends to be greeted with severe criticism; so much so, that when the Pope pleaded for Mary's help in uniting Christians at a gathering in 1982, some of Protestants called for a temporary suspension of all dialogues.[4] For Roman Catholics, calling for Mary's help as an intercessor is necessary for unity; for Protestants, the idea is divisive.[5] How divisive can a first-century young Jewish woman from an insignificant village be, when so much of the faith story of Christianity pivots around her answering favorably to God's call? Like that same story, how we interpret her role and her humanity becomes a matter of debate. This is not an argument about who has the right interpretation of Mary, nor indeed about the right to interpret Mary at all. Some things can be agreed upon easily: she said 'yes' to God; she was a mother; and her son became the Savior of the world. However, our various interpretations of her and her significance have shaped Protestant and Roman Catholic dialogues. I argue that a number of interpretations can be used to benefit dialogues with Protestants.

LUTHER'S MARIOLOGY AND LATER LUTHERAN MARIAN TEACHINGS

To gain some understanding of the difficulties Protestantism has with Mariology, the sixteenth-century Reformers are a logical place to start. But they themselves are not consistent in statements about Mary or doctrines concerning her. There are a variety of reasons for this, including their contexts, their formative theologies, and evolution in the reforming movements. Generalizations become difficult. Between Lutherans and Anglicans, for instance, one needs to consider the Mariologies of medieval continental Europe and England, where different influences and teachers emerged. Their teaching on Mary reflected numerous factors creating, distinguishing, and deepening identities within a theological tradition.

Luther, for instance, is an example of these conflicting directions. First, having been a part of the Augustinian order as a monk, priest, and professor, he would have experienced "first hand the impact of the Virgin

---

3. Meyer, "Ecumenical Unburdening," 681.
4. Ibid., 682.
5. Ibid., 682.

Living Traditions

and the Saints on the spirituality he personally adopted."[6] Although his thinking would evolve, Luther maintained devotion to Mary throughout his life. In his early days, he would have practiced the piety of his time, which was "dominated by Mary and the saints, who were central to the system of merit and the search for salvation."[7] It would have been very radical to think differently or to shift away from the taught status quo. Even after Luther began proposing reforming theologies within the church, his personal retention of devotion to Mary was a deep part of his identity as a now-evangelical Catholic and reformer. As he would have been taught, Mary was considered first among the saints, a position described as *hyperdulia* by Thomas Aquinas as a means of distinction from the lesser saints.[8] The position of bearing the God-child into the world was obviously seen as something much more than merely being a follower: such a conviction, in the face of her first-century context, would be radical in itself. Further, the position presumed entitlement to a higher calling. Being the most directly associated with the humanity of Christ, Mary was logically thought to be worthy of such admiration.[9] Intense admiration may have become misdirected. Mary became something more than human, and as time passed, she lost more and more of her human nature. Recalling his time as monk, Luther would speak disdainfully for "placing such trust in a saint rather than in Christ."[10] Even so, he also could not deny her role in his faith formation.

In time, Luther's own faith formation and his personal Mariology changed. Over the course of his life, he understood Mary as a receiver of God's love and favor, and his objection was to giving her the title of mediator and intercessor. While he retained a personal use of the *Hail Mary* prayer, he did so by teaching that the prayer is meant not to be a prayer to Mary or to invoke her, but as a prayer of meditation on the grace of God placed upon her.[11] He objected to her playing a significant role in the salvation of humankind, which was also part of his opposition to the teaching that the merits of the saints could be added to Christ's own to save us from sin. The belief in Jesus as the ultimate judge of all people prevented Luther from seeing how a saint, even the woman who bore Jesus into the world,

---

6. Brooks, "Lily Ungilded," 137.
7. Kreitzer, "Luther Regarding," 249.
8. Brooks, "Lily Ungilded," 136.
9. Kreitzer, "Luther Regarding," 250.
10. Ibid., 252.
11. Johnson, *"One Mediator,"* 230.

could intercede or influence divine decisions. Mary needed Jesus' salvific presence in the world as much as any faithful person. He argued in his commentary on the *Magnificat* that it was no wonder people had made an idol of her. If they had "stressed her low estate, and in so doing, have marveled at the abundant grace of God," the people would have seen the great riches of God bestowed upon her as a person of faith, not as a person elevated to a supreme position.[12]

Like other Reformers (even those who differed from his teaching), Luther did not question any of the Marian dogmas taught by the church. Instead, he adopted the ones that could be found in Scripture, such as the Virgin Birth and Mary as *Theotokos* or God-bearer.[13] The official church teachings that placed Mary in positions where Luther thought they lessened faith in God and Christ, however, had to be replaced and discarded for the sake of the gospel.[14] For Luther and the early Reformers, the symbolic Mary represented "God's being made fully human in Jesus Christ, without which there would be no salvation for humankind, in accordance with the ancient and honored dictum."[15] Anything less than this was not satisfactory to Luther, as it would have missed the focus of the dogma, namely that Mary's exaltation did not exclude or replace God's Incarnation,[16] and it did not elevate her to a special status. Mary's status was an exemplary sign of God's grace and mercy in creation.

What Luther and other Reformers objected to most were the perceived abuses of Marian dogma, but these abuses were not seen as Church dividing, given Mary's role in the Christian story.[17] There was a very clear and positive understanding of Mary's role in salvation history, and no doubt that she played a significant role in the gospel, and thus in the creeds. Yet devotion to her was seen as adiaphora, so Luther explicitly taught that devotion to Mary should not get in the way of remembering Christ and remembering the poor.[18] If anything, she should remind the faithful of their call and actions in identifying themselves as believers. Here we see a component of Lutheran theology: authentic Lutheran thought and spirituality

---

12. Brooks, "Lily Ungilded," 140.
13. Meyer, "Ecumenical Unburdening," 683.
14. Kreitzer, "Luther Regarding," 253.
15. Meyer, "Ecumenical Unburdening," 685.
16. Ibid., 685.
17. Ibid., 683.
18. Ibid., 684.

tends to focus on the incarnational and sacramental. It is not humankind that seeks to discover God, but it is God who became human in order to discover humankind.[19] Both Mariology and Marian devotion must have their source in this thinking, so Lutheranism can accept them as part of Lutheran identity and practice. To do otherwise is to deflect or cloud the genuine sign of incarnation.[20] Mary is the example of grace bestowed, and so for Protestants she can be placed amongst all the other biblical and post-biblical figures who also have received grace, albeit to a lesser degree.[21]

Luther's focused position on Mary has more in common with the Orthodox Christian view of the *Theotokos*, Mary as the Mother of God, rather than with the Roman Catholic view of her as intercessor. Luther retained her importance as the Theotokos even though he did come to reject other medieval titles given to Mary, such as "Queen of Heaven" and "Mother of Mercy."[22] He stressed this because of the lack of evidence for such titles in Scripture. As a result, the early Lutheran Reformation had both a "biblically based *Theotokos*-dogma using the Mariology of the ancient church, and it had a Marian piety and devotion based on this dogma, taking its bearings from the soteriologically interpreted notion of God's condescension."[23] Luther believed that as the second person in the Trinity, Jesus was incarnated in Mary's womb, so that, as a human being, Jesus was born of Mary. This corresponds well with the title of *Theotokos*. Lutherans thus confessed in the Formula of Concord in the Solid Declaration, Article VIII.24:

> On account of this person union and communion of the natures, Mary, the most blessed virgin, did not conceive a mere, ordinary human being, but a human being who is truly the Son of the most high God, as the angel testifies. He demonstrated his divine majesty even in his mother's womb in that he was born of a virgin without violating her virginity. Therefore she is truly the mother of God and yet remained a virgin.[24]

While this article and declaration come forty years after Luther's death, it is obvious that his position was still influential.

---

19. Ibid., 686.
20. Ibid., 686.
21. Ibid., 687.
22. Kreitzer, "Luther Regarding," 258.
23. Meyer, "Ecumenical Unburdening," 688.
24. Kolb and Wengert, *Book of Concord*, 620.

Present day Lutheranism is not as devoted to Mary as its founder. Present day Lutheranism sees Mariology as practiced by Roman Catholics as questionable, given what they see as confusing the unique place Christ occupies in our salvation. The constructed parallels between Mary and Christ, such as her Immaculate Conception and assumption into heaven are viewed as disrespectful to the *Theotokos* doctrine.[25] While adhering to their position of Mary as mother, Lutherans cannot attribute the position of intercessor to her. To appoint her in a position where she has spiritual and pastoral authority over Christ is against the Lutheran understanding of salvation and justification.

ANGLICAN MARIOLOGY

Anglican Mariology evolved differently, yet has similarities. Because the Roman Catholic ideologies and teachings were also enforced in England, it makes sense that various practices and devotions would be the same. As did Luther and other Reformers, Anglicans honored Mary as the *Theotokos*. However, because of the breadth of Anglican thought and theology today, ranging from high Anglo-Catholic to low evangelical, some Anglicans actively avoid honoring Mary beyond the position she holds as the mother of Jesus, retaining the terminology of veneration as opposed to devotion or reverence. When those who went into exile during the reign of Mary Tudor returned during the reign of Elizabeth, Calvin's influence actively shaped the breadth of Anglican theology.[26] In a vein that would be crucial to Protestant identity in England, he taught that all prayer addressed to Mary was blasphemous because "she needed Christ as much as do all other human beings."[27] Over the centuries, particularly following the Reformation, a number of doctrines pertaining to Mary have been critically evaluated because of critical interpretation of Scripture that have countered the validity of these doctrines, especially in the eyes of evangelical Anglicans. Despite the broad objection to seeing Mary as an intercessor, certain Anglican traditions, especially those in the Anglo-Catholic orientation, have permitted direct address to Mary and other saints.

The English Reformers did emphasize Mary's role in the Incarnation, so she was accepted as the Mother of God from both a scriptural and a

---

25. Meyer, "Ecumenical Unburdening," 689.
26. Nazir-Ali and Sagovsky, "Virgin Mary," 132.
27. Ibid., 133.

traditional position. They also accepted, like Luther, her perpetual virginity, but they never affirmed or denied her preservation from original sin as claimed in the doctrine of Immaculate Conception. That said, since 1561 the Anglican Church has had certain feast days ascribed to Mary: the Conception of Mary, the Nativity of Mary, the Annunciation, the Visitation, and the Purification. The feast of her Assumption was eliminated as Scripture did not support it, and it would have elevated her to the same position as Christ. But in the breadth of Anglican tradition, this feast has been restored as her Falling Asleep. In some ways, Anglican practice is reactionary.[28] After the suppression and dismantling of the various medieval sources of Marian devotion, Mary's place in Anglican doctrine is surprisingly intact.

Both the English and Continental Reformations rejected Mary as intercessor or mediator alongside Christ. Like their Lutheran contemporaries, the English Reformers emphasized Scripture as the standard for faith, so Jesus was understood as the only mediator between God and humankind. Any devotion to Mary where she appeared as the mediator was heavily discouraged. The reintroduction of Mary into church prayers and the continuance of the *Magnificat* in evening prayer became prominent less than one hundred years after the Reformation in England. However, her roles as mediator and intercessor never regained popularity outside Anglo-Catholicism.

MARIOLOGY IN DIALOGUE WITH ROMAN CATHOLICS

There are three things at issue between Protestants and Roman Catholics on how to celebrate and honor Mary: the nature of revelation, relation of Scripture to tradition, and the nature of the Church.[29] This is consistent with both traditions' identities and faith formation, providing areas of fruitful engagement and discovery, despite their differences. Expressions of Mariology through the lens of soteriology, and vice versa, must consider these three areas. When Mary is the subject, the dialogue must have reference to all three; otherwise, it is bound to fail.[30] Misunderstandings have created a variety of problems within the dialogues, but have also created avenues for exchange of ideas and room for clarity. Such exchanges and clarity ought to come with an agreed vocabulary and understanding

28. Ibid., 131.
29. Fannon, "Protestant Approach," 121.
30. Ibid., 121-22.

of what various terms mean in partnership. Keeping a discrete silence on whether the discussion on Mary is suitable for ecumenical dialogue is not longer viable.[31] To maintain that silence would be make her the proverbial elephant in the room.

There is no direct place in Lutheran liturgy for Mary, or for any other saint, to be viewed or used as a mediator between ourselves and God. Commemorating their example can be highlighted in a feast day observance or included in the intercessory prayers, but the challenge would be the distinction between a direct address and an invocation. Philipp Melanchthon intimated that intercession and invocation "need to be distinguished from each other," and so, while Lutherans do believe that honoring the saints should be both allowed and sought, invoking them to act on our behalf is to be rejected.[32] If, from the Lutheran perspective, the invocation of Mary is one of Christian freedom and choice, then a Lutheran Christian is quite within his or her choice to move away from the classic position of idolatry and come to appreciate Roman Catholic practice.[33] In liturgy, piety, and theology, the Lutheran tradition follows Luther's lead. Yet it is obvious that Mary's significance in those three areas has declined to a point where it cannot be supported by the same traditional Lutheran avenues.

The early Lutheran tradition included a place in devotional life for both meditation and ascription of honor to Mary, but there seemed to be little place for the same in the recent Lutheran-Roman Catholic dialogue,[34] where Mary (or at least discussion about her) has become a source of befuddlement. Since it was a part of early Lutheranism, it would not be out of line to expect certain prayers, like the *Hail Mary,* to be retained in present day Lutheranism.[35] If it is true that Mary occupies a valued place within Lutheranism, then any conclusion has to be more than Lutherans recognizing "Roman Catholics who venerate and invoke Mary and the saint are not idolaters; and that Lutherans need not venerate and invoke Mary and the saints in order to be in closer communion with Roman Catholics."[36] There is also a counterpoint: if it is true that Mary occupies a valued place within Lutheranism, then any acknowledgement must not include a forced

31. Flanagan, "Marian Theology," 352.
32. Persaud, "Lutheran Perspective," 60.
33. Johnson, "One Mediator," 237-38.
34. Ibid., 230.
35. Ibid., 231.
36. Ibid., 226-27.

Living Traditions

compromise leading to a confessional debate on denominational identity.[37] The two are connected, valid, and logical positions on the spectrum of reception.

At one point in Lutheran-Roman Catholic dialogue, Mariological discussions were not unheard of, and were even encouraged and found to be productive. In 1967, Arthur Carl Piepkorn proposed that agreement could be reached on a number of Marian related topics, especially her *fiat mihi*, the example of "empowered response that God elicits from all those of His children whom He calls to be in freedom workers together with Him."[38] Yet by 1992, such discussion had disappeared. In the Lutheran-Roman Catholic document *The One Mediator, The Saints, and Mary*, Lutherans are not asked to declare anything positive about how the invocation of Mary and the saints contributes to the liturgical, ecclesial, or spiritual life of the faithful. They are not asked to compromise or to accept anything that would be contrary to their respective theologies, especially that of justification. They are, however, given opportunity to repeat protests, fears, and reservations from the time of the Reformation.[39] Since Mary is referred to in prayers and hymns of the Lutheran tradition, something must have occurred to change positions between 1967 and 1992. If, then, Marian issues are not church dividing for the Reformers, but certainly are for contemporary Lutheranism, how should this be approached ecumenically? More importantly, what caused such a dramatic shift in twenty-five years?

One argument is directly connected to the ecumenical movement's own evolution during this time. The Second Vatican Council ended with a call to greater unity and dialogue between denominations and within the World Council of Churches (WCC). The reception of this call forced a discussion for clarity on highly divisive issues like baptism, Eucharist, and ministry. Over the course of fifteen years, ending with the publication of the watershed document, *Baptism, Eucharist and Ministry* in 1982, many theologians, both lay and ordained, were actively engaged and discussing areas of agreement. The WCC called for its various denominational members to respond.[40] Lutheran responses were varied, but all called for serious self-reflection and self-examination of the various theologies and doctrines that had caused the divisions in the first place. This exercise caused some

37. Ibid. 227.
38. Piepkorn, "Mary's Place" 80.
39. Johnson, "One Mediator," 227.
40. Thurian, "Introduction," 1-4.

denominations, such as the Anglican Church of Canada, to rediscover and recover some traditions, theologies, and histories.[41] Thus, their identities as particular and individual denominations would become clearer. To understand themselves in dialogue, a denomination would need to be self-aware as a collected body. The denomination would need to be strong, yet flexible in their identity as "X" in order to engage in dialogue with a denomination that would also need to be strong, yet flexible in their identity as "Y." If this line of thinking is correct, the Lutheran protest against Mary being described as anything other than the *Theotokos* becomes part of Lutheran identity. It does not mean that Mary becomes lesser in Lutheran theology; she becomes different from the Roman Catholic understanding. There are areas of agreement, but to go further would involve an evolution in Lutheran theological identity that is not possible given existing practices of Lutherans.

For Anglican-Roman Catholic dialogue, an agreement was reached in the 2005 document, *Mary: Grace and Hope in Christ*. As in Lutheranism, there is a significant importance placed on matters held in common with Scripture. As a result, there are significant concerns "about the uses of Scripture for theology that are to be kept in mind when exegeting and interpreting relevant biblical passages."[42] Differences in these would obviously causes different views of Mary to arise. Article Six of the Thirty-nine Articles, describing what is contained in Holy Scripture as divine revelation, is also "directed against any tendency to promulgate as essential to faith teachings"[43] anything that cannot be supported by Scripture itself. This, too, can lead to difficulties in the dialogue, but it has been less problematic than with Lutherans.

Church traditions do not invalidate scripture, but scripture can invalidate church traditions. Agreement about Mary (or any other doctrine or teaching for that matter) will not be reached by appealing to anything beyond what is found in scripture. Given the priority of the Word in Protestantism, Roman Catholic dialogues will not benefit or grow from adding to scripture. This would suggest to Protestant partners that scripture is insufficient, which is contrary to key Protestant doctrine. No one would suggest the same thought applies to Roman Catholics, as church teachings are believed to enhance one's understanding of scripture. But there is a

---

41. Ibid., 28-9.
42. Borsch, "Mary and Scripture," 376.
43. Ibid., 376-77.

distinction. Just how important is total agreement on the subject of Mary within Protestant-Roman Catholic dialogue, when there are many other pressing issues for discussion and ongoing matters of difference? Perhaps a better question to ask: why do the areas of agreement matter less than the areas of difference?

MARIOLOGICAL POSSIBILITIES BETWEEN PROTESTANTS

Mary, a biblical figure mythologized to the point where her humanity is lost and misidentified as passive or absent, becomes the means for the restoration of authentic identity. She is more than a "yes," more than a womb. She is someone who knew social injustice well because she lived it. She raised her son to see social injustice, the people affected, and those involved in creating the injustices. Her existence in the story of faith speaks to her necessity in that same story: without her, the role and value of women in salvation history would be lessened if not erased from memory. The piety encouraged by the Reformers in sixteenth- and seventeenth-century England promoted two perspectives: one, to see Mary as "sharing fully in human experience;" and two, to see her "as participating in salvation history."[44]

Sharing in human experience means to see Mary as woman, wife, and mother. There is a tendency to forget that Mary was a mother. Given our overall social tendency to forget the mothering presence, this is hardly worth noting. It is, however, worth bringing out of the dark recesses of our minds. Mary was a mother, who had birthed a son, who would have fed and nurtured him, clothed him, cleaned him up when he soiled himself or fell, kissed him good night, and loved him in a way only mothers of sons can understand. She would have taught him his Jewish faith, taken him to temple and synagogue, explained customs and traditions to him, answered his endless toddler questions of why. Her "yes" consisted of a commitment to raise a child, a boy, in a community and society that favored him over her. Her mothering raised the Savior of the world.

Mary can bring Protestants together by asking about identity. How do we understand our dialogue partners and how are we coming across to them? Are there historical or cultural assumptions being made outside of the theological discussions that are hindering our abilities to agree? We are challenged to consider how we are interpreting, misinterpreting, and presuming we have the "correct" interpretation. Mary, and our interpretations

---

44. Nazir-Ali and Sagovsky, "Virgin Mary," 134.

of her and her role in our faith story, challenge us to examine ways we are looking to correct, rather than to listen to what is being said. If we can forget something as simple as her actual motherhood, focusing solely on her "yes," we can also neglect other angles of understanding the same texts.

Participating in salvation history means to see Mary as "a willing participant in God's redemption of the world."[45] She asks us about our purpose. How are we answering God's call? With a yes, a maybe, a no? Are we responding with joy and with trust, despite our fear of uncertainty or social judgment? Are our fears of uncertainty and judgment preventing ministry and frustrating the work of the Spirit? How are we responsible to God's call by way of continued action? Are we responding and then failing to trust in the subsequent results because those results are not what we expect, or are costing too much of our resources? From some scholastic and traditional accounts, Mary was an adolescent when she said, "yes." Whether she was a young adolescent or an adult, it makes no difference to the reality of her being unmarried and pregnant, a social status of subsequent rumor and disgrace in her community. The Bible does not record for us her doubts, her loneliness, her sadness, or her frustration.[46] Scripture only says that after the birth of her son, Mary pondered all these things in her heart. If we say "yes" to God's call, that "yes" comes with the responsibility to carry it through in spite of our doubts, our fears, and our being overwhelmed.

Considering this, Mary also asks us about our preconceived notions. Who are we as faithful persons, as followers of God, as stewards of creation, as engaged dialogue partners? Who are we when we engage in dialogue: hesitant or confident? Are we prepared for the challenges that come from being in ecumenical relationship with another denomination? When we are presented the gift of ministry, of mutuality, of meeting each other as we are, Mary's example confronts us with the reality of our disunity.

What are our spiritual practices and devotional life like? Are we Sunday-only Christians, only-in-an-emergency Christians? When do our faith practices impact our lives? Who are our examples and role models? Some Protestant traditions tend to look to the Reformers for inspiration before looking to the saints. What would it be like if the saints, such as Mary, were just as inspirational as the Reformers? It is possible to be devoted to Mary and to still be Protestant, but there is a final barrier to cross.

---

45. Ibid., 134.
46. Luke 2:19, and again Luke 2:51, following the time of Jesus at the temple.

Living Traditions

Academic treatments of the issues don't necessary solve the divisions among us. The pew can be a very difficult barrier to cross due to set beliefs and set traditions. The pew is also a place where theologians of all walks begin, so how we talk about Mary and other issues will have an impact. Very few people outside the academic world know about the agreements their denominations have agreed to. This is an opportunity to teach, to learn, and to discover what is meaningful and troubling to congregants, and thereby to become better dialogue partners. It is also an opportunity to learn that some of what is discussed has very little to do with theology as a discipline, and more to do with how to live a faith filled life. If Mary were presented as the feisty social justice advocate, as her song entails her to be, having her as a role model is not threatening to Protestant identity. Mary would remain in a place of reverence in the story of faith, as she always has, but she would not be seen as docile or the sweet quiet role in the annual pageant. She would be seen as a teacher, instructor, mother, and rebel; as defiant, assertive, strong, and an advocate. In most cases, only one of those words has come down to us at the expense of the others.

There is something about Mary, and as we continue to learn from her, she changes our perspective on everything personal, ecumenical, and denominational.

BIBLIOGRAPHY

Borsch, Frederick H. "Mary and Scripture: A Response to Mary: Grace and Hope in Christ." *Anglican Theological Review* 89, no.3 (2007):375-99.

Brooks, Peter Newman. "A Lily Ungilded? Martin Luther, the Virgin Mary and the Saints." *Journal of Religious History* 13, no.2 (1984):136-49.

English, Leona M. "Roman Catholic Solutions to the Marian Question in Anglican-Roman Catholic Dialogue." *Journal of Ecumenical Studies* 37, no. 2 (2000):142-50.

Fannon, Patrick. "The Protestant Approach to Mariology." *Irish Theological Quarterly* 29, no. 2 (1962):121-35.

Flanagan, Donal. "Marian Theology in the Ecumenical Discussion." *Irish Theological Quarterly* 33, no. 4 (1966):352-57.

Johnson, Maxwell E. "*The One Mediator, the Saints, and Mary*: A Lutheran Reflection." *Worship* 67, no.3 (1993):226-38.

Kolb, Robert, and Timothy J. Wengert. *The Book of Concord: The Confessions of the Evangelical Lutheran Church*. Translated by Charles Arand, Eric Gritsch, Robert Kolb, William Russell, James Schaaf, Jane Strohl and Timothy J. Wengert. Minneapolis, MN: Fortress, 2000.

Kreitzer, Beth. "Luther Regarding the Virgin Mary." *Lutheran Quarterly* 17 (2003):249-66.

Lutheran Church in America. "Response." In *Churches Respond to BEM*, vol.1. Edited by Max Thurian. Geneva: World Council of Churches, 1986.

McKnight, Scot. "The Mary We Never Knew." *Christianity Today* 50, no.12 (Dec 2006):26-30.

Meyer, Harding. "The Ecumenical Unburdening of the Mariological Problem: A Lutheran Perspective." *Journal of Ecumenical Studies* 26, no. 4 (1989):681-96.

Nazir-Ali, Michael, and Nicholas Sagovsky. "The Virgin Mary in the Anglican tradition of the sixteenth and seventeenth centuries." In *Studying Mary: Reflections on the Virgin Mary in Anglican and Roman Catholic Theology and Devotion: The ARCIC Working Papers*, 131-146. Edited by Adelbert Denaux and Nicholas Sagovsky. New York: Continuum/T&T Clark, 2007

Persaud, Winston D. "A Lutheran Reflection on *The One Mediator, The Saints, and Mary* in Relation to the Question: How Do Lutherans Understand Prayer for Other People?" *Dialog: A Journal of Theology* 52, no. 1 (2013):58-65.

Piepkorn, Arthur Carl. "Mary's Place Within the People of God According to Non-Roman Catholics." *Marian Studies* 18 (1967):46-83.

Thurian, Max. "Introduction." In *Churches Respond to BEM*, vol.1. Edited by Max Thurian. Geneva: World Council of Churches, 1986.

7

Tillich for Today's Church
The Critique and Gift of the Spiritual Presence
Andrew O'Neill

UNTIL THE ADVENT OF the stethoscope, the human body was a black box. A doctor of the nineteenth century could take a family history and perhaps take the pulse of his patient, but was able to do little other than treat presenting symptoms like fever or "hysteria." Today, with advances in medicine and science, we know that a symptom like fever is not a disease in and of itself, but indicates an underlying condition.

Much has been written about the presenting symptoms of the mainline Western church: declining membership, continued disunity in the body, dwindling numbers seeking ministry as a vocation. Yet what if we are incorrectly identifying these conditions as disease, rather than symptoms of a deeper underlying condition? Or what if the metaphor itself is deficient, and these challenges to the contemporary church are not problems to be solved, but critiques from which to learn more about the underlying (human) condition?

With a longer memory of the Reformation in mind, we can recall that the Spirit of God has always spoken a word of critique in order to reshape the church in the image of God's promised kingdom of justice and peace, rather than the image of our favored tradition. Here, I want to be more specific about the nature of the church's necessary self-critique, and equally necessary self-transcendence. To do this, I want to first consult the great twentieth-century theologian and diagnostician of the human condition, Paul Tillich, a theologian whose titanic contribution is woefully underrepresented in Canadian seminaries today. Specifically, I want to highlight how Tillich's concepts of theonomy and the Protestant principle encourage the church toward self-critique. Second, I consider how Tillich, and his Canadian theological inheritor, Douglas John Hall, employ the biblical symbols of cross and kingdom to describe the way in which the church must also transcend its particularity. Whereas Tillich's concept of the Spiritual Community widens the scope of God's activity beyond congregation and denomination, Hall's later concept of the *ecclesia crucis* helps the church in the West name the loss of institutional privilege as *gift*, rather than defeat. Finally, I point to a contemporary theological approach that emphasizes the Spirit's constructive presence and to the language of ecumenical dialogue as gifts offered to the continual and mutual work of reformation.

BEGINNING WITH TILLICH

Trained as a Lutheran pastor and forced to leave Germany in 1933, Tillich emigrated to the United States and wrote almost exclusively in his adopted language of English until his death in 1965. Read widely both within and outside seminaries, much of Tillich's writing focused on how the kerygma of the Gospel, which he called the "message," was a healing and reconciling response to the brokenness and finitude of the human condition, or "situation" of life and history. Tillich's magnum opus is his three-volume *Systematic Theology*, published in 1951, 1957, and 1963. Briefly, in the first volume of *Systematic Theology*, Tillich first sets out his project of correlating philosophy and theology, and second, does so in his most well-known concept: God as being-itself, or the "ground of being." Comprising both being and non-being, being-itself is the source and possibility of all things. Within the divine essence, the dialectic of being and non-being are perfectly balanced. Within human existence and history, their imbalance is at the root of the universal experiences of estrangement, ambiguity, and anxiety. Humankind, so encumbered by its finitude, is unable to bridge the gap between existence and essence. In the second volume of *Systematic Theology*, the revelation of the Christ, or what Tillich calls the New Being, is an historical revelation of the reunification of being and non-being. The New Being repairs the breech between divine essence and human existence. Once experienced, the historically revealed Christ becomes a transhistorical or eternal possibility throughout life and history. In the third volume, the Spiritual Presence is identified with this continual revelation and with the work of reuniting essence and existence, not only in the individual now, but also in the Spiritual Community. Where the cross is the theological symbol of the historical event of the New Being, the kingdom of God is the theological symbol of the promised fulfillment of all life. In this paper, I focus on Tillich's concept of the Spiritual Presence as it relates to the constant reformation of the church and of God's people.

SELF-CRITIQUE: THEONOMY AND THE PROTESTANT PRINCIPLE

In *The Religious Situation of the Present Time* (1926), amid despondency following the First World War, Tillich wrote optimistically about the possibility of the *kairos* moment—an eruption of the new, the Unconditioned, within history, but unconditioned by it—which can bridge the gap between what is and what ought to be.[1] Later, in *The World Situation* (1945), Tillich wrote that optimism in an epochal moment in history had yielded to an existential void.[2] Economic depression and a return to war had caused the hope of *kairos* to give way to crisis, what Tillich calls the anti-*kairos*. The anticipated eruption of the unconditioned is replaced with the very real possibility of history coming to an end through a complete dissolution of society.[3]

In subsequent postwar writings, Tillich is especially critical of fundamentalisms which insist on the authority of church teachings, but which are ultimately unable to respond to deep currents of crisis. For example, Tillich describes churches in the wake of the First World War that rejected cultural and political revolutions, as rebellious expressions of secular autonomy. In return, these churches were repudiated as antiquated for asserting a transcendent heteronomy.[4] The result was mutually destructive of both religion and culture. The church cannot "relapse into the mere reiteration of tradition," or neo-orthodoxy, as a response to crisis.[5] A living theology must account for revelation in a way that does not render human reason and

1. Richard, "Tillich's Analysis," 126.
2. Ibid., 130.
3. Ibid., 132.
4. Tillich, *Protestant Era*, 61.
5. Tillich, "World Situation," 193-94.

experience redundant.[6] A church that is too quick to consecrate aspects of its culture, however, is equally in jeopardy. Here, Tillich cites the interwar church, which lacked the power to respond to spiritual and cultural crisis because it had become an instrument of nation and economy.[7] As a human institution, the church has at different times participated in the feudal order, nationalism, war, the illusion of peace, and the bourgeois ideal of property, without transforming or transcending them.[8] Thus, he says, "the first word . . . to be spoken by religion to the people of our time must be a word spoken against religion."[9] And yet, for Tillich, religion remains "the state of being grasped by something unconditional, holy and absolute."[10] Theology that offers serious critique of the church is not merely interested in debasing it according to its flaws, but in repairing it according the ultimate *telos* of revelation.

As opposed to the self-grounded autonomy of reason, or the imposed heteronomy of religious or state law, Tillich offers theonomy as "reason united with its (revealed) depth". Theonomy is "the demand that everything relative become the vehicle of the absolute and the insight that nothing relative can ever become absolute itself."[11] It is "the innermost law of humanity, rooted in the divine ground which is humanity's own ground."[12] In the first volume of *Systematic Theology*, Tillich distinguishes theonomy from the authority of religion or of the church. Revelation judges religion—as well as history, culture and reason—because it ultimately seeks the sacrifice of conditioned manifestation to its unconditioned truth. In the second volume of *Systematic Theology*, he identifies this with Jesus, who is described as "the Christ . . . who sacrifices what is merely 'Jesus' in him" in favor of revealing the unconditional in God.[13]

God's self-revelation in Christ offers the shape and possibility of estranged humankind's reunion with its unconditioned ground of being.[14] Because the Christ is revealed under the conditions of existence, however,

---

6. Tillich, "What is Wrong?"
7. Tillich, "World Situation," 192.
8. Tillich, *Protestant Era*, 181.
9. Ibid., 181-82.
10. Ibid., 65.
11. Ibid., 53.
12. Ibid., 63.
13. Tillich, *ST* 2, 134.
14. Parrella, "Tillich's theology," 74.

Living Traditions

human reason and agency are not overwhelmed, but the chasm between the world as it is and the world as it should be remains. Religion, culture, and art, even when ultimately concerned with God's self-revelation, can only offer finite responses to what is infinite. The challenge for the church, especially, is how to offer the critique of revelation while also being subject to it.

The exemplar of theonomy manifest in the church, for Tillich, is the Protestant Reformation, during which the crisis of a particular confessional and cultural identity was transcended through a self-critical, and no less faithful, examination of revealed mission and purpose.[15] Although identified with a particular historical context, the principle of a self-critical theonomy is not limited to the Reformation, nor to any one religious form or period, but arises whenever a stand is taken "against the attempts of the finite and conditioned to usurp the place of the unconditional in thinking and acting."[16]

SELF-TRANSCENDENCE:
THE SPIRITUAL COMMUNITY AND THE ECCLESIA CRUCIS

Critiques of the church, then, are based not in taste, trend, or favor, but in Tillich's concern for the unconditioned, for the infinite, for divine essence, to be revealed. The immanence and transcendence of God is a paradox that defines many of Tillich's central theological symbols.[17] God as being-itself roots human existence within the unconditioned ground of being, yet this is revealed within history, under the conditions of existence, in Jesus the Christ.[18] The kingdom of God is a symbol that expresses both the inner-historical transformation of life and history, and also the transhistorical, transcendent *telos* or fulfillment of life and history.[19]

The immanent experience of the divine within life and history is the province of the Spiritual Presence, the mediator of humankind's continued spiritual experience of transcendence.[20] The Spirit transforms even conditioned and fragmentary moments of transcending finitude

15. Tillich, *Protestant Era*, 239.
16. Ibid., 240.
17. Stenger, "Being and Word," 287-88.
18. Tillich, *ST 3*, 144.
19. Tillich, *ST 3*, 358-59.
20. Tillich, *ST 3*, 144.

into opportunities for spiritual freedom, diminished reliance on law, and other-mindedness.[21] Such spiritual experiences inevitably call people into community.[22] The community called by such experiences, however, is not synonymous with the church. What Tillich calls the Spiritual Community is concretely "manifest" in the church universal and its local churches, but it is also present wherever and however individuals and groups seek holiness, truth, and justice.[23] The church can be both a concrete-historical location of transcendence, and that which must, by times, be transcended: "The Church, properly conceived, is not a religious community but the anticipatory representation of a new reality." [24]

The primary symbols of this new reality are the Christ and the kingdom. Together, these eternal symbols shape the self-critical and self-transcending identity of the church by speaking to the transformation of life and history without being subject to their distortions.[25] "A church which raises itself in its message and its devotion to the God above the God of theism without sacrificing its concrete symbols," Tillich writes, "can mediate a courage which takes doubt and meaninglessness into itself. It is the Church under the Cross which alone can do this."[26] The kingdom to which the cross points stands outside of history as an image of reconciliation, of existence reunited with essence, where estrangement and ambiguity have been subsumed. It also stands within history as possibility and *telos*, as the concrete goals of peace and justice. It is through these symbols, and not according to whim or trend, that the church can both be aware and critical of its mission and faithfully communicate hope in the midst of crisis and change.

Like Tillich, Douglas John Hall also describes his cultural era as being in crisis. However, for Hall the crisis is not entirely tragic. He describes the decline of the church, at least in the West, as occurring over a much longer period of time than merely recent decades. The loss of institutional and narrative privilege is the result of centuries of challenges to claims of intellectual and ethical authority. He describes a church mired in denial and

---

21. Stenger, "Being and Word," 291-92.

22. Parrella, "Tillich's theology," 79.

23. Tillich, *ST 3*, 152ff. Wherever the church is not "concretely manifest," Tillich refers to it as "latent."

24. Tillich, *ST 3*, 243.

25. Tillich, "The Problem," 16.

26. Tillich, *Courage to Be*, 178.

disbelief. The church of today is struggling to come to terms with a reversal of expectations, not so much concerning its message, but of its mission and methods of shaping community.[27] For Hall, this is also a source of great hope and possibility. The church that does not deny its loss of privilege, but participates in it knowingly and joyfully, is liberated to the Gospel and to renewed mission. Death and renewal are the shape of the *ecclesia crucis*: the church shaped by sacrificing the conditioned in favor of revealing what is unconditioned.

In his development of the concept of the *ecclesia crucis*, Hall notes that neither Jesus of Nazareth nor the cross of the Christ claim finality for themselves, but inevitably draw the individual out of self-concern, into relationship with the community.[28] The cross ultimately reveals "God [who] suffers with the world," thereby expressing God's compassion for and solidarity with the world, and concern for the world's future.[29] Only a church that stands with the afflicted, not from a position of privilege but from a posture of humility, is capable of communicating and embodying a new reality. The church of institutional privilege—membership, authority, establishment, influence—is less exposed to the scandal of this message. While it may reach out to those in need, a privileged church risks less than those with whom it stands. The church of diminished privilege is compelled to reflect critically on its mission and purpose; to seek partnerships with other groups within that wider Spiritual Community who also manifest justice and peace; and to stand with society's victims.[30]

Seen from this perspective, the decline of the institutional church is not a failure in its mission, but a theonomous critique of the inherited privilege that has brought it to this point. Consequently, the church's decline is not an anti-*kairos*, a dissolution in the face of an existential void or absolute end. Rather, it can be understood as a *kairos* moment. As the church surrenders its particularity and transcends the last vestiges of membership, authority,

---

27. Hall, *Confessing the Faith*, 201.
28. Hall, *Waiting*, 101.
29. Ibid., 83.
30. One example of this is The United Church of Canada's 1986 apology to aboriginal victims of a state-sponsored and church-operated school system (the "Indian Residential Schools") that, from 1876 to 1996, sought to rid indigenous peoples of their culture and identity. The potential legal and financial cost of issuing an apology for Residential Schools was uncertain, but predicted to be grave. The apology, however, helped to initiate extended societal conversation in Canada, resulting in the creation of the Truth and Reconciliation Commission, whose official mandate concluded in 2015.

and privilege, it finds courage in its concrete symbols of transformation and self-transcendence. The religious situation of our day is not one of tragedy, but of hope.

MARKS OF THE SPIRITUAL COMMUNITY

There are two contemporary approaches to church transformation that I think exemplify the idea of surrendering particularity. The first such approach is beautifully described in Ben Quash's "found theology." The problem he sets out is how to hold what is "given" or known—for example, a liturgical tradition or theological position—not as immutable, but as a gift of the Holy Spirit; and how to respond with similar grace to what is "found" or new. Given and found are mutually and dynamically related; one never overwhelms the other.[31] The brilliance of Quash's approach is that the Spirit is understood as present in both moments, in both what is given and what is found, and encourages imagination. Here, imagination does not make an idol of invention or ingenuity, but instead assumes that what has been and what might be meet in a moment of mutual consideration. "The God who has 'stocked our backpack for the journey' also 'places things in our path' up ahead."[32] Quash calls this unique gift of the Holy Spirit its "spirality"—that is, its persistent creativity in every moment which is to come.[33]

A practical, but no less imaginative, approach to critique and transcendence is embodied in the intent and language of ecumenical conversation. In my eight years as member and co-chair of the Anglican-United Church Dialogue in Canada, we regularly tried to describe our differences as both "gifts" and "encouragements." As denominational partners, we would describe the gifts of another denomination—usually traditions or ways of thinking and being—as providing sparks for our own denomination's self-reflection. Similarly, we would offer encouragements in the form of observations from experience or areas of theological divergence, which offered our partners an opportunity for reflection and creativity. Gifts and encouragements are discerned with the Spirit, and are meant to be supportive of the work of the Body. They are never meant to be directives for change, and certainly not condemnations, but opportunities for renewal. As with "found theology," the operative assumption of all ecumenical work

---

31. Quash, *Found Theology*, 18.
32. Ibid., xiv.
33. Ibid., 29.

Living Traditions

is that the Spirit is at work in us and others. To put it in terms familiar to Tillich, the self-critique and self-transcendence of the Spiritual Community happens as a community, recognizing difference as a strength, and identity as multi-faceted and dialectical.

Of course, the real value of wrestling with the givenness of our traditions, both theologically and ecumenically, is borne out not only in clarifying identity and community in the Body of Christ, but in how this affects our shared mission. The current phase of the Anglican-United Dialogue is concerned primarily with how the two traditions can more closely cooperate on outreach and stewardship. In practice, we are once again discovering that our mission is not shaped by our community, but rather that our community is shaped by our mission. The Moderator of The United Church of Canada and the Primate of the Anglican Church of Canada, together, acknowledged in 2017 that our shared identity is nowhere more important than in our work on the recommendations of the Truth and Reconciliation Commission[34]. Here, once again, the revelation of God's vision of peace and justice faces us with the question of how we will communicate the message of the Gospel into today's situation.

BIBLIOGRAPHY

Hall, Douglas John. *Confessing the Faith: Christian Theology in a North American Context.* Minneapolis, MN: Fortress, 1996.

———. *Waiting for Gospel: An Appeal to the Dispirited Remnants of Protestant "Establishment."* Eugene, OR: Cascade, 2012.

Hummel, Gert and Doris Lax, eds. *Being versus Word in Paul Tillich's Theology.* Proceedings of the Seventh International Paul Tillich Symposium 1998. Berlin: De Gruyter, 1999.

Manning, Russell Re, ed. *The Cambridge Companion to Paul Tillich.* Cambridge: Cambridge University Press, 2009.

Parrella, Frederick J. "Tillich's theology of the concrete spirit." In *The Cambridge Companion to Paul Tillich*, edited by Russell Re Manning, 74-90. Cambridge: Cambridge University Press, 2009.

Quash, Ben. *Found Theology: History, Imagination, and the Holy Spirit.* London: Bloomsbury T&T Clark, 2013.

Richard, Jean. "Tillich's analysis of the spiritual situation of his time(s)." In *The Cambridge Companion to Paul Tillich*, edited by Russell Re Manning, 123-37. Cambridge: Cambridge University Press, 2009.

---

34. The Truth and Reconciliation Commission, as noted above, was a federally mandated process of disclosure of and response to the abuses that occurred within the Indian Residential School System that removed indigenous children from their families and sent them to residential schools in distant communities.

Stenger, Mary Ann. "Being and Word in Tillich's Doctrine of Spiritual Presence: Issues of Subjectivity and Relationality." In *Being versus Word in Paul Tillich's Theology*. Proceedings of the Seventh International Paul Tillich Symposium 1998, edited by Gert Hummell and Doris Lax. Berlin: De Gruyter, 1999.

Stenger, Mary Ann and Ronald H. Stone. *Dialogues of Paul Tillich*. Macon, GA: Mercer University Press, 2002.

Tillich, Paul. *The Courage to Be*. London: Nisbet, 1952.

———. "The Problem of Theological Method." *Journal of Religion* 27, no.1 (January 1947): 16-26.

———. *The Protestant Era*. Chicago: Chicago University Press, 1951.

———. *Systematic Theology*, 3 vols. Chicago: Chicago University Press, 1951-1963.

———. "What is Wrong with the 'Dialectic' Theology?" *Journal of Religion* 15, no.3 (Apr 1935): 127-45.

———. "The World Situation." In *Main Works*, Volume 2, edited by Michael Palmer, 165-96. Berlin: De Gruyter, 1990.

8

Luther, the Bible, and the Rule of Faith

Robert C. Fennell

ONE OF MARTIN LUTHER's most remarkable, emphatic, outrageous, and misunderstood claims was that the Bible is *perspicuous*—that is, essentially clear and not needing interpretation:

> I would say of the whole of Scripture that *I do not allow any part of it to be called obscure* . . . the Scriptures are *perfectly clear* in their teaching.[1]

Luther argued vigorously that the Bible, unadorned and uninterpreted, yields the riches of wisdom and knowledge that every theologian and—more importantly—every faithful believer needs. No interpretation is necessary, and especially not an official interpretation from the church.

But "perfectly clear" is not as straightforward it seems. Luther did not assume that Scripture's meaningfulness leapt spontaneously off the page towards any reader. On the contrary, the clarity of the Bible is only possible, as Luther understood it, because underlying all faithful and accurate reading is the *regula fidei*, the Rule of Faith. The Rule must be already at work, already limiting and shaping exegesis:

> For Luther, the Rule of Faith functioned as an interpretive assumption more than as an overt hermeneutical tool. While his language

---

1. Luther, *Bondage,* 129, 133 (emphasis added).

is at times inconsistent when speaking of the Rule of Faith, his reverence for the Rule within Christian biblical interpretation is clear and unwavering.[2]

Luther's sense of the Rule of Faith was idiosyncratic—a function of his particular formation, convictions, and situation—but it functioned just as the Rule had for centuries before him. The broad content of the *regula fidei* is stable over time, but in practice (for Luther as for countless others), there is a variety of applications of the Rule. It is, as Mickey L. Mattox puts it, "the faith given in the church" that is always "intrinsic to properly Christian exegesis."[3]

Luther's views about the essential clarity of Scripture are liberating. He called for freedom, independence from ecclesial domination over interpretation, and (in one sense) a great deal of personal autonomy. To stay focused only on these perspectives, however, would be distorting. Luther anchored his thinking about the Bible in a broad theological heritage that was profoundly authoritative for him. In the eyes of the ancient and medieval theologians, on whose shoulders he stood, interpretation is not a wild, unregulated thing. There must be a relationship to a greater community of faith and practice. Luther was deeply invested in a communal reading strategy, as seen in his insistence "that all spirits should be proved *in the sight of the church*."[4] In other words, private interpretation on its own will not yield a faithful and accurate reading of the Bible. In short, we must discern meaning "according to a definite code."[5] Interpretation is not a merely personal matter; it ought to happen within the community and among the learned; and it needs to have recourse to a common reliable standard. This standard is the Rule of Faith.

Luther was deeply concerned for the health, vitality, and faithfulness of the church. While he is remembered as a reformer, Luther did not set out to grow a new branch of the Christian tree. Rather, he sought the renewal of the one church from within. Luther's overarching goal to draw all believers into greater faithfulness to Jesus Christ is deeply compelling. It was through the encounter with Scripture that he believed this to be possible. Both doctrinal fidelity and the comfort and instruction of God's faithful people are founded upon sound interpretation of the Bible. Here I want to

2. Giere, "'As a Bee,'" 40.
3. Mattox, "Luther's Interpretation," 56.
4. Luther, *Bondage*, 125 (emphasis added).
5. Ibid.

Living Traditions

focus on the way the Rule of Faith governed his exegesis, because I share his conviction that accessing the ancient sources of the faith are essential to the renewal of faith.

When Luther used the terms "analogy of faith" and "rule of faith," he linked them to Paul's turn of phrase in Rom 12:6, "in proportion to faith" (in Greek, *kata tēn analogian tēs pisteōs* = "according to the 'analogy' of his faith.") Luther adopted the expression to refer to a normative constellation of doctrines and practices that shape and govern Christian thought, including the sacraments of Eucharist and baptism, prayer, and the wisdom of Scripture. Luther assumed that, like him, his readers would have prior catechetical formation in the Christian essentials that would be so ingrained as to form a habitual, "ruled" way of reading the Bible. It was for this reason he could be assured that for them as for him, the Bible's meaning was always "perfectly clear."

In this chapter I briefly review Luther's background, then turn to explore the shape of Luther's sense of the Rule of Faith and the ways in which he applied it to exegesis via two quite different writings: his *Commentary on Galatians* and *The Bondage of the Will*. As exemplars of Luther's hundreds of published works, they serve well to illustrate how his approach to Scripture functioned within the Rule of Faith.

LUTHER'S BACKGROUND AND CONTEXT

As a young man, Luther intended to study law. A dramatic experience during a lightning storm, however, made Luther resolve to enter the Augustinian order. The Augustinians nurtured Luther's intellectual gifts and furthered his education. Without a doubt, his deep and sustained faith formation within this monastic order reinforced in him a communal and "ruled" practice of engaging the Bible. Although he left the Augustinian order when his conflict with Rome escalated in 1518, Luther always retained an inner spirituality and identity deeply formed by the order of monastic life, which thoroughly rooted him in the essentials of faith and theological practice.

As a prolific author and keen lecturer at the University in Wittenberg, Luther believed his service to Scripture to be his principal service to Jesus Christ. As an antidote to what he saw as the errors of late medieval theologians and the Roman Catholic Church, Luther worked intently to make the Bible come alive and to ensure that his theological contribution was thoroughly biblical. Still, as Mark D. Thompson remarks, "Luther's thought did not emerge in a vacuum. Even at the points at which he is most creative and insightful, there are echoes of the centuries which preceded him."[6] Luther was keenly aware of his debt to earlier generations, yet distrustful of the scholastic tradition that had dominated medieval theology and his own education. He calls the scholastics "smug and idle," persons who offer "foolish and wicked glosses."[7] Nevertheless, he favored the dialectical scholastic method of reviewing opposing positions before settling on his conclusion.

Another important feature of Luther's theological context was the Quadriga, a medieval approach to interpretation. This model elaborated a four-fold sense of Scripture: the literal-historical, allegorical-spiritual, tropological-moral, and anagogical-eschatological meanings of each passage. Outlining the four senses was *de rigueur* for medieval readers, but Luther insisted that it is only the first sense (the literal-historical) that is of any real importance: "no allegory, tropology, or anagogy is valid, unless the same truth is expressly stated historically elsewhere."[8] He perceived the drive to allegorize every part of the Bible as deeply distorting. The best reading, Luther held, was always the literal: that is, the "most obvious and simple meaning of the text," which still included typology.[9] Thus while Luther's remedy for the illness of allegory was to emphasize the literal-historical or obvious plain sense of the words, he still assumed a passage may properly be seen to have more than one layer of meaning. This is possible to perceive and interpret if one has a sound and properly formed Christian theological foundation within the Rule of Faith.

A final element to take into account in Luther's intellectual context is humanism, which provided the urgently important tools of accurate Bible translation and philology. These enabled Luther to give close attention to the grammatical elements in the biblical text and therefore to the subtle differences in meaning that can result. Humanist scholarship also provided access to non-Christian classical texts, and to new critiques of the Roman Church and traditional theology. From Luther's point of view, however, humanists placed too much emphasis on human agency and pagan thought. In contrast, he grounded his teaching in Scripture as the best of all sources

---

6. Thompson, *A Sure Ground*, 2.
7. Luther, *LW* 26:122.
8. Luther, *LW* 10:4.
9. Harrison, "Hermeneutics," 349.

Living Traditions

of theological wisdom, and secondarily in the Church Fathers of the early Christian centuries. The exegete's task is not finally to dig about in word studies, but to discern and especially to *proclaim* the Word as it is ever being disclosed through the text. In practice, Luther strove to confirm the believer's experiential confidence in God's promises.

LUTHER'S RELATIONSHIP WITH TRADITION

Beyond his immediate context, Luther had an ambiguous relationship with the historic tradition of the church. He despised slavish obedience to it, and adamantly insisted that the Bible stands well above human tradition. Yet he also held a critical affinity for his forbears in the faith. Luther did not perceive himself to be an innovator: "we do not invent any new understanding, but we adhere to the analogy both of Holy Scripture and of the faith."[10] He persistently claimed to represent Christian doctrine faithfully and truly. In 1518, at a hearing before Cardinal Cajetan, the papal legate sent to investigate and discipline him, Luther insisted,

> I am not conscious of having said anything contrary to Holy Scripture, the church fathers, or papal decretals or their correct meaning. All that I have said today seems to me to have been sensible, true, and catholic.[11]

His teaching and convictions, in short, he believed to be entirely orthodox. Any view of his implementation of the Rule of Faith must take into account how deeply embedded he was in the tradition of the ancient church. At the same time, his use of the Rule was both *plastic* (freely composed from the tradition) and *elastic* (flexible). He added and subtracted doctrinal emphases, corrected the errors he saw, and had an expansive view of the power of doctrine to guide both interpretation and Christian living.

Despite his robust insistence that the Bible is perspicuous, Luther acknowledged that from time to time, there were still some difficulties with the text. Tradition provided helpful clues as to how to proceed. Luther began with Irenaeus's and Augustine's principle that the clear parts of Scripture help to interpret the parts that are less clear: "If words are obscure in one place, they are clear in another."[12] Put another way, Scripture is its

---

10. Luther, *LW* 2:16.
11. From "Proceedings at Augsburg, 1518," *LW* 31:263.
12. Luther, *Bondage*, 71.

own interpreter. Here again however, the infrastructure of the Rule of Faith is immediately needed, for in Luther's mind, the meaning of clear parts of Scripture is obvious *only* to those who have been catechised and are firm in their faith in Jesus Christ. Luther aligned himself with the tradition expressed in the ancient ecumenical creeds and councils of the church, regarding them as a sure guide to the truth. To the Apostles' Creed he added the Athanasian Creed, the *Te Deum laudamus*, and the Nicene Creed as the best examples of the church's creedal statements.[13] Luther called Nicaea, Constantinople, Ephesus, and Chalcedon "the four great principal councils," chiefly because of their fidelity to the core Christological doctrines they defined.[14] Despite that high regard, Luther saw no special authority residing in ecclesial councils. Rather, it was the consensus articulated by the councils (via the creeds) that is the touchstone against which all exegesis must be tested.

Also fundamental to Luther's "plastic and elastic" treatment of the Rule of Faith were the ancient Fathers of the church. It was the Fathers, after all, who first set down the Rule. But it is difficult to come to a single conclusion about Luther's ambiguous relationship with the Fathers. On the one hand, he said, "Christ is a higher authority than the Fathers."[15] Whereas many had sought to make the teaching of the church an authority perhaps even higher than the Bible, Luther proposed the key principle for which he is justly famous: *sola scriptura*. That is, "by means of Scripture alone" is theology faithfully done. Luther never felt obliged to agree with the Fathers and indeed quarreled with them when they erred in their use of Scripture. He would not write a blank cheque to tradition: any teaching must be verified by Scripture before it can be approved. On the other hand, Luther often turned to the Fathers as allies. He made plentiful reference to Tertullian, Origen, Cyprian, Ambrose, Augustine, Jerome, and others, and it is clear that Luther valued them for their faithfulness to Scripture. He contended that the closeness in time of the patristic writers to Jesus' earthly ministry, and their keen understanding of the gospel, recommended their witness in an unparalleled way.

The magisterial authority claimed by Rome, on the basis of the tradition of the church, was unacceptable to Luther. At the outset of his public protest, from 1517 onward, he sought to reform the church from within.

13. Luther, *LW* 34:201–29.
14. Luther, "On the Councils and Church," *LW* 41:22, 118.
15. Luther, *Bondage*, 97.

Of primary interest to us is Luther's rejection of the Pope's supreme authority in biblical interpretation. In doing so, he openly challenged Western Europe's centuries-long reliance on the theological rulings of the Roman Church and its hierarchy. "What can the Church settle," he asked, "that Scripture did not settle first?"[16] Yet without the Roman magisterium as the primary arbiter of biblical interpretation, would just *any* interpretation do? Luther's emphatic response was "no." The Rule of Faith must be engaged, for interpretation can never be a matter of personal opinion. Rather, it must cohere with the faith of the whole (true) church: "wherever and by whomever some meaning *which does not conflict with the rules of faith* is brought forth, no one should reject it or prefer his own."[17] This doctrinal coherence of the Rule—the boundary points, as it were—was fundamental and urgent to Luther.

LUTHER'S SENSE OF THE RULE OF FAITH

Despite Luther's comprehensive examination of Scripture, we can only find slivers of occasional notes on how he approached interpretation. Premodern interpreters did not share the modernist preoccupation with detailed methods for biblical studies. Luther, true to the habits of his age, simply interpreted the Bible in ways that were coherent and obvious to him. He assumed that his exegetical method would be transparent to his readers. Yet this transparency was possible only because Luther presumed that his readers would already know the Christian faith and its core doctrines—the Rule of Faith. He trusted that his readers would already be "inside" the community of Christian faith and practice.

Luther used both "rule of faith" and "analogy of faith" to denote essentially the same thing. As noted above, Rom 12:6 ("according to the 'analogy' of his faith") was his reference point. This rule or governing analogy was a normative constellation of doctrines and practices that shape and govern Christian thought, including the interpretation of Scripture. Therefore those who understand the Bible rightly, he wrote, "are those who know the rule and analogy of faith . . . those who in fear test all things according to the analogy of faith."[18] The Rule (or analogy) of Faith is immediately practical when sorting through possible allegorical interpretations, for example,

---

16. Luther, *Bondage*, 69.
17. Luther, *LW* 10:462 (emphasis added).
18. Luther, *LW* 16:246.

or the conflicting views of various interpreters. In addition to the dynamic relationship to tradition, as discussed above, we can say that there are three distinctive hallmarks to Luther's sense of the Rule: its public character; its correlation to the creeds; and its doctrinal grounding in Scripture itself.

The Rule of Faith is public. Luther conceived of the Rule of Faith as a matter of public record. As he wrote to Erasmus, "there is no need to revere hidden mysteries, since no doctrines in fact are such."[19] He regarded all doctrine of any worth to be fully grounded in the public testimony of Scripture. Elements of the Rule—such as the sacraments, the gospel, the confession of Christ, the person and work of the Holy Spirit—are the heritage of all Christians. Accordingly, the work of interpretation is understood as public, properly occurring only within the communal body of believers.

The Rule correlates directly to the creeds. Luther clustered together a number of elements he assumed as axiomatic within the Christian way of believing. In one place he wrote of "all the other items which the whole world has received as articles of faith."[20] He pointed, casually but confidently, to elements of the common Christian faith that he presumed to be normative and self-evident for everyone within Christendom: "This we know; for *the Creed which we all hold* runs thus, 'I believe in the holy catholic church.'"[21] Luther assumed his reader would know the context and meaning of that line from the Creed, and, by extension, would understand the important bearing of the whole Creed upon what he was saying.

The Rule of Faith is doctrinally grounded in and derived from Scripture itself. Underlying all of Luther's explorations of Scripture were the theological preunderstandings that he found deeply embedded in Scripture itself. But it is precisely *how* he reads the Bible that interests us here: how he draws his theological conclusions as he reads the text. Within two of his works, *The Bondage of the Will* and the *Commentary on Galatians*, we can see six biblically grounded doctrines that formed the theological platform on which Luther undertook his exegetical work:

- Christocentrism
- Justification
- Faith
- The nature of God and human nature

19. Luther, *Bondage*, 98.
20. Luther, *Bondage*, 127.
21. Ibid., 120 (emphasis added).

Living Traditions

- The reality of Satan and his antagonism to God's purposes
- Pneumatology.

Together with Christian practices like the sacraments, prayer, and public worship, these doctrines form the constellation of the Rule of Faith that guided Luther's biblical interpretation. These were the raw materials that he had internalized and that functioned together as a matter of habit in his exegetical work. Drawing attention to a handful of doctrinal commitments, as I do here, is not meant to imply that these are fully comprehensive of Luther's system of thought, or that other elements are unimportant. Rather, these elements simply serve to illustrate the main contours of Luther's appropriation of the Rule of Faith.

Christocentrism

Above all else, Luther's Christological understandings funded virtually everything he had to say. Prime among all his evaluative criteria was whether a statement speaks of Christ—"propels" or "urges" (*treiben*) Christ—to God's people. This consequently emerges as the controlling factor in Luther's interpretation of all Scripture: "For this much is beyond question, that all the scriptures point to Christ alone."[22] It was the key to unlock the door to understanding everything in both Testaments. The revealed Christ is the main theme, subject, content, and perspective of the Bible as a whole, when read through faithful Christian eyes. Luther was not the first to take this position: it was a common assumption for most Christians of the preceding centuries. The significance lies in the frequency with which Luther returned to it, and the prominence he gave it in his exegetical work.

Just as Christ is the key to the Scriptures, then, Christocentrism is the key to understanding all of Luther's theology. Luther understood Jesus Christ as did most of the Christian tradition in all the preceding centuries: as the Son of God, born of the Virgin Mary, truly human and truly divine, who suffered and died on the cross as the one who provides the grace that all persons require for forgiveness. Luther was squarely within the ancient and orthodox Christology that the Rule of Faith delineated. Above all, "Christ is Lord over Scripture and over all works. He is the Lord of heaven, earth, the Sabbath, the temple, righteousness, life, sin, death, and absolutely

---

22. Luther, *LW* 35:132.

everything."²³ Christ is also Lord of the church and unmistakably Lord of Luther. In the 1535 introduction to his lectures on Galatians, Luther signaled his unswerving emphasis on this bedrock doctrine that undergirded all his interpretive work: "in my heart there rules this one doctrine [*iste unus regnat articulus*], namely, faith in Christ. From it, through it, and to it all my theological thought flows and returns, day and night[.]"²⁴

This term—*articulus*—gestures toward the articles of the Apostles' Creed specifically, and more generally to the Rule of Faith that Luther presupposed his readers held in common with him. *Articulus* is a cipher for a whole matrix of interrelated, prior doctrinal commitments: "I have perceived and noted in all histories of all of Christendom that all those who have correctly had and kept the chief article of Jesus Christ have remained safe and secure in the right Christian faith."²⁵ So when Luther came to the biblical materials, he brought a Christology that was already fully formed, and that stood as the cornerstone of his interpretive practices: "Take Christ from the Scriptures—and what more will you find in them?"²⁶

Christocentrism guided Luther's exegesis in pragmatic ways. When a text was "rather ambiguous" (such as Gal 1:6), he focused the interpretation through a Christocentric lens.²⁷ Later, in evaluating Paul's teaching about righteousness by faith rather than by the law, he made a Christological comparison: faith is "diffused throughout the works [of a human being] in the same way that the divinity is throughout the humanity of Christ."²⁸ This concept of the "diffusion" of divinity and humanity in Jesus is predicated on the ancient Chalcedonian definition about the hypostatic union: two natures that concur simultaneously in the one Jesus. In this, Luther again revealed the normative status of the Rule of Faith to which he adhered. It is the person of Jesus Christ, as well as the effect of his saving work, that are vital and central to how he approached the text. But Christology was no mere principle. This is a Person, the One in whom Luther had lodged his personal trust and obedience.

---

23. Luther, *LW* 26:295.
24. Luther, *LW* 27:145.
25. Luther, *LW* 34:207.
26. Luther, *Bondage*, 71.
27. Luther, *LW* 26:47.
28. Ibid., 266.

Justification

Luther's notes on the first two chapters of Galatians turned upon the problem of justification: how sinful human beings are made right with God. Some see justification as the main feature of Luther's revolutionary theological contribution. He himself identified it as "the rule of faith[:] that we are justified by the grace and mercy of God."[29] Thus to his exegesis of Galatians Luther brought his prior conviction that justification is only and always the free gift of God, made available to us by faith in Jesus Christ. Good works and good behavior have no part in the formula. However, these convictions do not leap spontaneously out of the text of Galatians: *Luther held them to be true before he began his exegesis.* Consequently his analysis of Paul's teaching about justification in Galatians depended on the Rule of Faith already formed in him.

So much turned on the hinge of the doctrine of justification in Luther's theological system that he urged it upon his readers as an essential doctrine. "This is the chief doctrine of the Christian faith," he wrote, "for in it are included all the other doctrines [*articuli*] of our faith; and if it is sound, all the others are sound as well."[30] Luther emphasized this doctrine again and again, insisting on it as a matter of life and death that must urgently be understood.

In exploring Gal 3:10, Luther concluded that Paul and Deuteronomy are "in complete conflict" about the Law and its impact on righteousness: Paul wrote, "'Whoever does the works of the Law is accursed.' Moses [wrote], 'Whoever does not do the works of the Law, is accursed.'"[31] Like most alert readers of the Bible, Luther was aware of such contradictions in Scripture. His answer to riddles like this is precisely the Rule of Faith, which provides normative doctrines—like justification—to govern faithful interpretation: "No one understands this passage unless he has the correct doctrine of justification."[32] By invoking that core doctrinal conviction about justification, Luther shows his hand. *Doctrine* is the interpretive instrument, the code-breaking device for sorting out whatever difficulties Scripture presents.

---

29. Luther, *LW* 17:114.
30. Luther, *LW* 26:280, 282, 283.
31. Ibid., 252.
32. Ibid.

Faith

In exegeting Gal 3:6, Luther wrote of faith as the highest virtue. Faith is the means by which we receive God's gift of grace, given through Jesus Christ. It is under this heading that Luther's famous distinction between faith and works should be understood. Salvation as a whole is entirely a gift, and thus works do nothing for us. Again, it is essential to note here the Christocentric shape of Luther's sense of the Rule of Faith. In commenting on Gal 3:10-11, Luther offered an excursus on the significance of faith,[33] exploring its nature by reading intertextually through a range of biblical materials: the letter to the Hebrews, the story of David, the example of Abel. In all cases, it is the work of the Holy Spirit in the believer that makes possible a right understanding of the Bible. Luther said that only works specifically motivated by faith and a heart in alignment with God's purposes are any good. Reason, on the other hand, is at odds with faith. Luther's attack on reason was not obtuse disregard for a God-given ability, but rather a vigorous rejection of the overconfidence in reason and human capacity that he found among the scholastic theologians.

The nature of God and human nature

Luther's affirmations about the nature of God and human nature were intrinsic to his major reforming breakthrough concerning justification and faith. First among these claims concerned God's power, "without which we cannot see or do anything at all."[34] God's will "cannot be resisted, altered, or impeded."[35] The traditional divine attributes of justice, kindness, grace, steadfastness, and love were without question for Luther. He regarded them as axiomatic and obvious. Just as confidently, Luther held a rather dim view of human nature. He shared with Paul and many ancient and medieval theologians a notoriously pessimistic theological anthropology. In particular, Luther did not think much of human spiritual and moral capacities. From his perspective, human beings are not, by nature, capable of anything *except* sin, let alone good works, right belief, and accurate biblical interpretation.

---

33. Ibid., 248-270.
34. Luther, *Bondage*, 133.
35. Ibid., 80, 84.

In his remarks on Galatians, Luther declared that while we have an innate awareness of the divine, it is incomplete. The self-disclosure of God in Jesus Christ, as it is revealed through Scripture, provides the saving knowledge we otherwise lack. Given that our salvation "is utterly beyond [our] own powers, counsels, efforts, will, and works," we are completely reliant upon "the will, counsel, pleasure, and work of Another—God alone."[36]

Luther's thoroughly pessimistic view of human nature stood in contrast to the typically optimistic anthropology of the scholastic tradition, in which human beings were understood to be capable of at least some love for God, and thus participate, if only minimally, in their own salvation. From Luther's perspective, only in full awareness and confession of one's sin can one hope to find grace. Nevertheless, he wanted to reserve some dignity for the human being, both as a child of God and as a redeemed and justified creature with tremendous liberty. Humans are not merely animals, but are given conscience and freedom. So while human nature on its own is wholly insufficient, humans do have the ability to give allegiance to God, who is a better teacher. The atoning death of Jesus Christ then overrides the consequences of sin for human beings. Christ—not our works or wisdom—is the source of our righteousness. In this light, Luther considers human beings as *simul peccator et justus*, that is, simultaneously both sinful and justified by God in Christ.[37] Newfound liberty in Christ not only frees one *from* the consequences of sin and death and bondage under Satan, but also frees one *for* acts of mutual service and love. Care for the poor and love of neighbors then find their proper place as the outflow of a life graced by God's gift of justification. This is the vocational core of every human being, for all are called to serve.

The reality of Satan

Luther's conviction about the reality and influence of Satan is sometimes overlooked. Yet he referred time and again to Satan's existence and (false) power, and to his antagonism to Christ, God's purposes, and Christians: "it is undeniable that the devil lives, yes, rules in all the world . . . we are all subject to the devil . . . day and night he prowls around, seeking to devour everyone individually."[38] Satan's opposition to human welfare and to God

---

36. Ibid., 100.
37. Luther, *LW* 26:232.
38. Luther, *LW* 26:190, 192, 193.

exacerbates the sinful situation of human beings. Yet Satan's power is finally ineffective against God's sovereignty. He tries to prevail against God's purposes but is consistently thwarted by the power of Christ. Satan is especially at work in attempting to distract us from Christ's efficacious work and in trying to have us seek righteousness through our own efforts.

Satan's efforts are doggedly persistent: "God and Satan are personally . . . laboring to destroy the works and subvert the doctrines of the other, like two kings laying waste to each other's kingdoms."[39] One of the casualties within that battle is our capacity to hear and understand the Word in Scripture. On our own, we err and distort the revelation that God desires to impart. Yet God permits Satan's rule of this world in order to drive us to a frantic appeal to God's mercy. God's response, as Luther saw it, is expressed in the closely interrelated trio of doctrines (Christology, justification, and faith) that we reviewed at the beginning of this section.

Pneumatology

Finally, it is by virtue of the inhabitation of the Holy Spirit that human beings receive regeneration and the ability to interpret Scripture rightly. It is only the grace of God, mediated through the work and power of the Holy Spirit, which makes anyone able to believe and to understand. "The Spirit is needed for the understanding of all Scripture and every part of Scripture," since human capacities are invariably inept and inadequate for this task.[40] Without the Spirit, interpretation cannot help but go entirely wrong. Without the Spirit, the marks on the biblical page cannot point to the depths of divine reality. When it comes to grasping what God is imparting in Scripture, "the Spirit of God within, the living Teacher whose teaching is life" gives the needed illumination.[41] God longs to give this gift of the Holy Spirit, and hearts must be open to receiving it.

CONCLUSION

Luther's remarkable claim that the Bible is always "perfectly clear" is only possible because of the shared doctrinal commitments that he presupposed

---

39. Luther, *Bondage*, 93.
40. Ibid., 74.
41. Ibid., 64.

his readers held. The debt to his formation, education, context, and the wider tradition is always in evidence. Although Luther rejected the authority of the Roman magisterium, in other respects his sense of the Rule correlated strongly with other "catholic" thinkers down through the ages, particularly in terms of his Christocentrism. Despite his revolutionary spirit, it would be a mistake to suppose that Luther reinvented the Christian faith. It is more to see him as a *transformer* rather than truly a reformer, at least in terms of doctrine. He always worked within a ruled, habitual way of thinking and interpreting that is characteristically canonical and creedal in its orientation.

Significantly, the elements of Luther's sense of the Rule were always grounded in Scripture itself, and not derived from non-biblical traditions such as popular piety or the rulings of popes and councils. It was not enough for a doctrine or idea to be generally believed; Luther held everything to the criterion of being attested in Scripture. "Show me in the Bible," we might hear him saying, "and then I will agree." The internal coherence of his application of the Rule of Faith lay in the direct reciprocity between the written word and the coalescence of the doctrines that Scripture taught to believers.

Finally, it is important to recall that Luther's principal interest in interpreting Scripture was pastoral. Above all, he sought to address the dilemmas and confusions that life presents, first by dismissing that which is false; and second, by lifting up the reassuring and sometimes surprising truth of God's grace and love in Jesus Christ. Christ the Word is explicitly available in the Bible, and so it is to Scripture that Luther turns his own and his readers' attention. Luther's exegetical work was consistently concerned with these core purposes: to encourage faithfulness among God's people, and to point toward the transformation of the self into the image of Christ. He contended that, by the grace of God, this is the goal of the Christian life. Our quest today to re-form the traditions of Christianity faithfully will be aided by similar commitments to embracing God's grace and love, and to seeking faithfulness as we live in Christ's Way.

BIBLIOGRAPHY

Giere, Samuel D. "'As a Bee Gathers Honey': The Rule of Faith in Luther's Interpretation of the Old Testament." *Currents in Theology and Mission* 41 (Feb. 2014) 39–44.

Harrison, Peter. "Hermeneutics and Natural Knowledge in the Reformers." In vol. 1 of *Interpreting Nature and Scripture in the Abrahamic Religions: Up to 1700*, edited by Jitse van der Meer and Scott Mandelbrote, 341–62. Leiden: Brill, 2008.

Luther, Martin. *The Bondage of the Will*. Trans. J. I. Packer and O. R. Johnston. Grand Rapids, MI: Fleming H. Revell, 1957.

———. *Luther's Works*. 55 vols. Edited by Jaroslav Pelikan et al. American Edition. Philadelphia: Muehlenberg and Fortress, 1955–86.

Mattox, Mickey L. "Luther's Interpretation of Scripture: Biblical Understanding in Trinitarian Shape." In *The Substance of the Faith*, edited by Paul R. Hinlicky, 11–57. Minneapolis, MN: Fortress, 2008.

Thompson, Mark D. *A Sure Ground on Which to Stand: The Relation of Authority and Interpretive Method in Luther's Approach to Scripture*. Paternoster Biblical and Theological Monographs. Carlisle, UK: Paternoster, 2004.

9

The Intimacy of Trauma
Musings of a Firefighter Chaplain on Trauma and the Theology of the Cross
Jeffrey Hosick

WHERE DO WE SEE Luther's "theology of the cross" today? It is everywhere, and especially in the pain and suffering of those who live through traumatic events. I see these moments up close. The incidents in the following stories are true, but the names and places have been changed to protect privacy.

THE STORY OF JACKSON

"911 dispatch to Fitchburg firefighters. We have a motor vehicle accident, car and truck with entrapment, 6292 Highway 202, Gardner. That's a motor vehicle accident, car and truck with entrapment, 6292 Highway 202, Gardner. Time is 19:14." The scene was dismal. A white Mazda was under a grain truck, struck head on. The car was crushed from the bumper to the back seat.

We knew the driver was dead. In these circumstances, the Royal Canadian Mounted Police accident reconstruction unit leaves everything as it is. There is no longer an emergency, and they start measuring. At this point, no one is on the scene except emergency personnel. Soon, several teens arrive on foot. Then I see a couple, Mark and Kelly, holding each other while they stand on a grassy knoll. I approached to offer a bottle of water. "No, it's OK," Mark replies. "We think it's our son in that car."

After a time, the teens gravitate to the couple. There was a pit party going on, they explained. The couple's two sons, Jackson and Daniel, had attended the party with their friends. The eldest, Jackson, leaving to get some music, took the car at the back of the line. One of the teens identified the car as hers. Jackson left the party, driving dangerously fast. He stopped at a corner and waited for a slow-moving car. He was already impatient when he pulled in behind the slow car. Quickly he blindly darted around it into the pathway of the grain truck. He and his brother Daniel were impulsive, reckless, and self-serving. They were known to the police for both defiant attitudes and reckless driving.

I stood with Mark and Kelly for hours. No one was able to do anything but wait. Marcus Borg calls the places where our hearts are open "thin places."[1] A thin place occurs when reality shatters the illusions of the world and thrusts us into a vulnerable reconsideration of all that we thought we knew as true. The outer world shifts to the inner world. Sometimes these thin places are wonderful places, as we are in an altered state, touched by things beyond the everyday life. Sometimes the thin places are horrible places. They take us into an altered state, crushed by things in everyday life.

Douglas John Hall distinguishes an Anglo-Protestant reformation from the Germanic Protestant reformation. In the Anglo-Protestant version, Reformers like Wycliffe, Calvin, Knox, and Wesley influenced the Netherlands, France, and the British Empire, including the USA and Canada.[2] They are dominant influences in our culture. Calvin, a lawyer by training, wrote his theology as a young man. It is crisp, pragmatic, and measurable, where grace makes up for shortcomings. Known as the "theology of glory" or "theology of light," it is triumphal and glorious, and the resurrection inspires us to good behavior. Luther, in contrast, influenced Germany, Scandinavia, and Eastern Europe. Luther was somewhat older and in a different stage of life than Calvin when he wrote his commentary on Romans. He didn't think much of the "theology of glory." Instead, he articulated the "theology of the cross," which makes room for the realities of suffering.[3] This is theology "in the dark." It focuses not so much on performance, but rather on the need for grace to traverse despair, depression,

---

1. Borg, *Heart of Christianity*.
2. Hall, *Cross In Our Context*, 14.
3. Ibid., 20.

anxiety, and broken relationships. Grace radically touches and is present to the human rawness shared by all of us, and it challenges us to embrace the intimacy of sharing that rawness.

For Mark, Kelly, the teens, and me, all efforts for efficiency, affirmation, positive self-talk, legislated goodness, and triumphalism are torched at a moment like that crash on Highway 202. What is left is us huddling together on a grassy knoll, raw, stripped of defences, and standing with the naked reality of pain, shock, and anguish. First responders on the scene have a job to do. When the job is done, they go home. The chaplain's job—my job—is to not rescue, but to listen, to stand, to be still. It is to be wounded, raw, and naked in that moment with those who suffer.

THE STORY OF DANIEL

"911 dispatch to Fitchburg firefighters. We have a MVA involving car and motorcycle with entrapment, 7227 Highway 202 in Gardner, in front of Tim Horton's. That's a MVA involving car and motorcycle with entrapment, 7227 Highway 202, in Gardner, in front of Tim Horton's. Time is 21:43."

To regular people, an emergency call like that sounds bad, but to us with experience, we understand what is being said. Entrapment means a person is stuck and can't get out. People on motorcycles don't get stuck on their bikes during a motor vehicle accident. The entrapment means the car. It means the motorcycle hit the car so hard, the people can't get out of the car. We assume the biker is dead.

Arriving on the scene, I see the biker on the ground, broken, with a man kneeling above him. Apparently, the biker was showing off: he pulled the front wheel of his bike off the ground. Since it was just after dusk and the headlight was pointing to the sky, the car pulled out believing nothing was coming. Collision was inevitable. As I approach, the man looks up. Mark, Jackson's Dad, quickly makes eye contact with me as he kneels over his remaining son, Daniel. "Jeff," he says, "this isn't fair."

How well does your theology work "in the dark?" This is an opportunity for the church. Society no longer seeks a religious system as much as it does connection during times of alienation, comfort in times of distress, grace in times of disgrace.[4] People are not looking for a philosophy, because

---

4. Hall points to religious triumphalism as a problem whose antidote is a community of faith that permits self-doubt and self-criticism as a vital role in the life of faith: "And if we want to understand why historic religions everywhere have been under duress

they have one already. They are looking for a meaningful experience in the midst of a non-meaning event. The meaningful experience does not come in the form of words, but rather through *presence*, a presence that shows up and chooses to be there with them, without blame, judgement, or ideology. That presence guides us slowly through healing to wholeness. The challenge for us is to not talk about it, but to do it.

THE STORY OF CHRIST

In 1517, Martin Luther was troubled by a religious system profiting on the needs of the people. The religious system was raising money for the building of the cathedral in Rome. The church was exploiting the grief of poor people, telling them they could buy salvation with their donation. Regardless of what Christians believe about the church, frequently the general public says they experience the church these days in the same light. Hall describes triumphalism as the tendency to present itself as a full and complete account of reality, leaving little room, if any, for debate or difference of opinion, and expecting adherents' unflinching belief and loyalty.[5] The wider public says they see Christians as exploiting their mental and emotional needs for unsavory purposes or a political agenda. If this is not Christianity's agenda, then Christianity's message is being lost.

The theology of the cross is not much loved. Its emphasis is on the story of Jesus in that moment of stunned silence. Encountering an experience of violence—raw, naked, helpless, and victimized—triggers in human beings a temptation to turn to the bright side as quickly as possible. This exemplifies the theology of glory that sees beyond the cross to emphasize only the resurrection. So, the question becomes: how many of us see the cross and cover ourselves with an ideology, a principle, a cause, or a course of action, that distracts us from fully feeling this suffering? I have often said, and believe so more than ever, that religion most often serves as a defense against God, more than a way towards God. In this way Christianity fails to see the relevant needs of the people it is to serve.

---

throughout the modern period, it is surely in large measure because so many human beings refuse almost intuitively to give a priori assent to any explanation of existence that asks for it on the basis of authority alone—on the basis, for instance of long establishment" (ibid., 18).

5. Ibid., 17.

Living Traditions

The theology of the cross sees brokenness as the end, the limit-point, of human ability. We can only wait for divine grace to act. Divine grace is found in the vulnerability of waiting and sharing pain, not the drama of injustice. It is found in sharing bewilderment, and not moving too quickly passed to quick pat answer. The power of the theology of the cross is the bond of being messed up together, which is very uncomfortable.

Luther accuses the theology of glory of claiming bad things to be good, and good things to be bad.[6] Claiming to be messed up is not seen as good in the eyes of the modern world even though it challenges us with reality we wish to not see. Saying we are not messed up is supposed to be affirming, but it is bad because it continues the denial and does not address the illusions which distract us from solving the problem. When problems arise, as in devastating car accidents, we find it difficult to stand with Mark and Kelly if we have not allowed ourselves to experience our own angst and imagine the angst of another. Rather than rush in and solve a problem we are not asked to solve; our task is to listen. The temptation to rescue ourselves from the ugliness of reality is encased in the rationalization that we are doing it for the betterment of the other. Essentially, we pass through the experience of feeling raw, naked, helpless, and victimized as quickly as possible, and we pass hurting people like Mark and Kelly in the process. We find it difficult to accompany them and stand with them as long as it takes them to recover. We fail to be present even to ourselves when our hope is lost, when we have needed a container to contain us.

There is an increased emphasis on trauma these days. People have experiences that have shaped them. It may not be car accidents, but each person carries a burden that is important. As a fire department chaplain, I have observed that firefighters live death and resurrection, experiencing it in a place without words. The church has the words, but often lacks the experience. Christianity is losing its relevance to society because people don't live in ideologies. They live with pain, suffering, abuse, and trauma. Trauma invites us to be messed up together, and from that place of chaos and confusion, we earn the right to be heard. When weakness and faint voices match another, we find community. The place of trauma is also the place of grace.

Critical Incident Stress Management, first developed by Jeffrey Mitchell, a former paramedic, was designed to find a way to break the isolation of stress through a structured conversation. Other approaches have followed,

---

6. Lull, *Martin Luther's Basic Theological Writings*, 30.

but the thrust is to develop an intentional community to deal with the impact of crises. Mitchell's model, designed for first responders, breaks the isolation through a series of questions. What happened? What were your first thoughts? What has the deepest impact? This is followed by an education phase about the symptoms and the expectations that arise in the aftermath of trauma. Through the structured conversation, group members turn from isolation to community. It builds a sense of belonging together in a team. This is also the main thrust of the theology of the cross: to form an intentional community built around being messed up, in pain, inadequate, and traumatized. All of these reflect the elements of the cross, as in Phil 3:10-12:

> I want to know Christ and the power of his resurrection and the sharing of his sufferings by becoming like him in his death, if somehow I may attain the resurrection from the dead. Not that I have already obtained this or have already reached the goal; but I press on to make it my own, because Christ Jesus has made me his own.

MY STORY

There is a pathway to this journey. In the fire service it's called Monday Night Practice. Monday night is the time to recognize incompetence and practice skills so that when a call comes Thursday midnight, we can be ready to perform. Correspondingly, the church is called to face the full limitations of human experience. Chaplains and others who serve the church are among the few who are invited into the rawness and nakedness of traumatic experience. For those who work with trauma, the equivalent of the fire service's Monday night practice starts with self-reflection in the room facing our own patterns, addictions, and illusions of how we avoid rawness and vulnerability. Then we ask very personal questions such as these:

> How many times a day do my ideologies fail me? Do I scramble to twist, bend, or stretch truth so I am not exposed? How often do I get busy with things that seem important, when in fact they are just distractions peppered with self-importance? How much do I use what I think of as good qualities, such as generosity, kindness, and niceness, as insurance policies so I won't be abandoned? Since I can spend lots of time convincing myself my forgeries are authentic, do I have the courage to remove my mask and see the

roundedness I am protecting? Am I willing to meet resistance from those anxious to not face this and stay hidden in their own illusions?

In the biblical story of the raising of Lazarus, (John 11) the usual assumption is that Jesus' healing powers are self-contained, always a resource for him to deploy through words, and actions to transform people and circumstances whenever he chooses. Yet the perspective of the power of the cross, offers another perspective. The powers of healing were not simply ready to be deployed but came as a result of his willingness to connect in each context of healing. Jesus' power to bring Lazarus to life emerged *because* he wept, and was willing to fully identify with Martha and Mary and to wait for grace to complete the task. That translates a challenge to us to fully identify and sit with Mark and Kelly until grace is expressed. We are challenged to see our own need for grace when we sit silently with those in anguish.

Luther's theology of the cross was first discussed five hundred years ago. It is at the heart of the Reformation, because the human heart is at the heart of the Reformation. The image of Luther's seal, otherwise known as Luther's Rose, bears the heart with a cross at its center. It asks: what happens when our hearts are broken? I believe our willingness to discover its expression in the modern context is the mission of the church.

BIBLIOGRAPHY

Borg, Marcus. *The Heart of Christianity.* New York: Harper Collins, 2003.
Hall, Douglas John. *The Cross in Our Context.* Minneapolis: Fortress, 2003.
Lull, Timothy, ed. *Martin Luther's Basic Theological Writings.* Minneapolis: Fortress, 2012.

10

"If Only—and Yet"
Luther's Legacy for Jewish-Christian Relations
Martin Rumscheidt

IF ONLY . . .

IF ONLY LUTHER HAD agreed to meet the man who had asked him to use his position and influence to support people seeking protection!

Let me offer a brief history lesson to set the stage. In August 1536, the Elector of Saxony and Luther's political ruler, Johann Friedrich, issued an edict (known today as an "executive order") prohibiting Jews from living in Saxony or to work there. He also made it illegal for Jews to travel freely in or through the land: no protective accompaniment would be granted them. The Rabbi of the Holy Roman Empire at the time, Josel of Rosenheim (1480-1554), who lived in Lower Alsace, wanted to plead personally to the Elector on behalf of his unprotected fellow Jews in Saxony.[1] Before doing so, he asked Luther, who had written a pamphlet in 1523 that spoke positively about Jews, to commend him to Johann Friedrich. The council of the city of Strasbourg had written a letter to Johann Friedrich asking the Elector to give protective accompaniment to Josel and to receive him.

---

1. I am indebted for the material on Josel of Rosenheim to the late Professor Leonore-Siegele Wenschkewitz and her article, "Josel von Rosenheim."

Living Traditions

In a letter dated 26 April 1537, the man who had brought Strasbourg into the Protestant Reformation, Wolfgang Capito, Luther's follow-reformer, asked the Wittenberg Reformer to receive Josel or, failing that, to forward Josel's supplication to the Elector and grant Josel an audience. Capito hoped that if Johann Friedrich had a change of heart, Jews might come to see that Christians showed compassion not only for strangers in their midst but also for those who, like Jews, were said to be their enemies. Capito entrusted a delegation to bring that letter to Wittenberg, having learned that Luther would not receive Josel of Rosenheim. Luther met with the delegation and engaged in a discussion that led them to be hopeful. Luther composed a letter to "my dear friend and beloved Josel" and gave it to the Strasbourg delegates to deliver to Josel and Capito. In it, he lays out the reasons why he could not put in a good word for Josel to the Elector. He wrote that he always was well disposed toward Jews and wished that they would be treated with kindness, and finally that he hoped that in His mercy, God would lead them to their Messiah. Then he adds that his good will is not to be interpreted as an affirmation of their errors. But if God were to give him time, he would write a little treatise with which, based on the testimony of the biblical prophets, he might convince Jews and win them over to their promised Messiah, who had come and lived among us and whose name is Jesus Christ.

That intended treatise appeared seven years later, in 1543. Other matters occupied Luther in between. One of those that needed his attention was a movement of Christians in Moravia who, having converted to Judaism, published a work that interpreted the Bible in a way that showed that the Christian faith has no basis in Scripture. His pamphlet repudiating that and other ideas of the movement, *Against the Sabbatarians,* is a prelude to the treatise that, as one would have to conclude, he believed God had given him the time to write. It is called *Against the Jews and Their Lies.* It contains the counsels Luther gave the ruling class in Germany for dealing with Jews and Judaism. I will name only three of them: "Burn their synagogues and make sure that nothing of them remains" (as the Nazis did in Kristallnacht, 1938); "Offer no protection to Jews and keep them off the streets" (as in the Nuremberg Laws, 1935); and "Make Jewish men and women earn their bread through hard labor" (as in my own father's company and its involvement in Auschwitz).[2]

---

2. I refer to the huge factory built and briefly put into operation, known as IG Farben Auschwitz-Monowitz. Its workforce consisted primarily of the inmates of the SS

I end this history lesson with an account of what was made of those counsels 403 years after Luther had published his promised treatise, which he believed God had given him the necessary time to compose. On 29 April 1946, at the International Tribunal in Nuremberg where Nazi government leaders were on trial, the publisher of the Nazis' hate journal *Der Stürmer*, Julius Streicher, was interrogated. He claimed that his motive had always been to enlighten rather than to instigate. His defense attorney asked him whether there had ever been other publications in Germany that addressed the Jewish question in a similarly anti-Jewish manner. With a smirk on his face, Streicher referred to a work by Martin Luther that he had on his bookshelf. He said that he had simply quoted from it, and added that if the honorable judges were only willing to look at it, surely they would have to indict Martin Luther as well. The work he referred to was *Of the Jews and Their Lies* (1543).

If only Luther had received Josel of Rosenheim! The Rabbi had read with approbation Luther's 1523 pamphlet *That Jesus Christ Was Born a Jew* in which Luther scolded his fellow-Christians for treating Jews inhumanely and called on them to show kindness towards Jews. What Josel read in its pages was something new, something unheard of: in the title of that pamphlet, Christianity's most precious word, Jesus Christ, was brought together with one of the most despised words of the Christian church: *Jew*. Josel and his fellow Jews did not need confirmation that the Bible was their people's work, but in a world that kept on denying this, Luther's affirmation opened a door between Christians and Jews. It appeared to them that it manifested understanding of the suffering of their Jewish fellow humans. There was genuine sympathy; it was not a calculated writing. Instead, here was a Christian speaking to Jews in a language filled with humaneness. Something dialogical was happening. But still, there is this sentence: "I will tell from Scripture what moved me to believe that Christ is a Jew born of a virgin and see whether I might perhaps entice many Jews to believe in Christ." One of the foundations of Luther's faith was "to tell from Scripture." For him, God lives in Scripture; God the Father of Jesus Christ speaks to him there. That is crystal clear and simple for Luther. Thus, the Jews also live in that same Scripture: "God has given the Holy Scriptures, that is the law and the prophets, to no other people than the Jews." So why don't they believe like him when it is so clear that it is in Scripture that Christ is to

---

extermination camp called Auschwitz-Birkenau.

be found? There is no question for him that what led him to faith can also bring Jews to faith.

Here a model becomes visible of a different order of rights between Jews and Christians on the foundation of the common ground of the Bible, at least for a moment. Luther spoke to Jews as fellow human beings, possibly even as sisters and brothers. "If the Apostles who were Jews had treated us heathens the way we treat Jews," he wrote, "no heathen would have become a Christian." And he adds that if there were a reincarnation, he would rather be born a pig than a Jew given the Christians' behavior toward Jews. The Reformer seeks the way into a new time, a time that no longer coerces Jews to accept the papacy, the church, and its incomprehensible teachings, but—free from coercion—lets them return to God's Scriptures. Come back, Luther says to Jews, to the faith of the prophets and patriarchs, and we will receive you with love. He is so sure, so unshakably sure, that the radiance of the old Scriptures will overcome not only popes, bishops, sophists, monks, and nuns, but also what he considers to be the Jews' blindness.

Luther is open to Jews; he is not open to Judaism. On their way home, the Strasbourg delegates opened the letter Luther had given them with his reply to Capito and the city fathers. We do not know what their reaction was when they read it. What we do have is a comment, recorded in Luther's *Table Talks* from 1540. Luther recalled that he had supported the request for safe conduct adding "for the sake of the name of Jesus Christ." The delegates supposedly said that the letter was good, but that an appeal to "the sake of the name of Jesus Christ" was an insult to them as Jews. They would rather pay for safe conduct than deliver such letters. The door had shut again!

Still, I believe that there is a crack in everything and that is where the light shines in, as the late Leonard Cohen put it.

AND YET . . . !

The Reformers of the fifteenth and sixteenth centuries, Hus, Luther, Zwingli, and Calvin—to name only the most prominent of them—put the Bible into the hands of the people, those whom twentieth-century writer Franz Fanon called "the wretched of the earth." They made Mary's song of praise in the gospel of Luke their hermeneutic: "He has brought down the powerful from their thrones, and lifted up the lowly; he has filled the hungry with good things, and sent the rich empty away" (Lk 1: 52-53). Then, and today, perhaps the most enduring legacy of the Reformation is the Reformers' conviction that it is the poor to whom the Bible as a whole addresses itself.

Once again, I offer a bit of history to set the stage for the next act. The late Rabbi Albert H. Friedlander of Westminster Synagogue in Knightsbridge, London, reports what happened when he gave a talk at one of the biennial gatherings of the German Kirchentag. He spoke about Auschwitz. During his address, people at the back of the hall were handing out flyers arguing that if people continued believing all that stuff about gas chambers that never existed, they who handed out those flyers would feel compelled to republish Martin Luther's *Of the Jews and Their Lies* so that Christians would finally come to see the truth that Luther told about Jews. To which Friedlander (may he rest in peace!) replied that the truth is rather that Christians must not abandon Martin Luther to people like that, that Christians and Jews alike must not let those dark views Luther had uttered about Jews become their sole way to measure the man and his work.

The achievement of Luther that I want to focus on here is that the Reformation of the fifteenth and sixteenth centuries put the Bible into people's hands and homes. John Wycliffe (1320-1384) had lit a flame that could not be extinguished. At the Church Council at Constance in 1415, Wycliffe was declared a heretic for several reasons, including his participation in translating the Bible. At that same council, another man who also had translated the Scriptures into the "language of the people" was declared a heretic and burned at the stake. His name was Jan Hus (1369-1415), a Czech priest and teacher who at Bethlehem Chapel in Prague preached in Czech to a standing room only congregation everyday (sometimes more than once) and would read them the texts of the Bible in their dialect. Luther, like Wycliffe and Hus, was later declared a heretic. He, who knew of those two fellow heretics and their translation work, knew of the power of biblical texts once they became accessible in the language "of the street" as he put it. Like them, he made the Bible accessible to a majority of people who could not read, write, or understand Latin, the only language in which the Bible was available. One can sum up that endeavor as follows. With Wycliffe and Hus, Luther carried the Bible out of the church into the fields and the streets where families lived. The Bible now was in the everyday hustle and bustle of village and town. The church would no longer be the sole source for the interpretation of Scripture. Every believer was empowered to read and to seek its meaning. What do those ancient texts say? What meaning do they have for us today? What do Christians who are ready to follow the voice of the

Master have to be attentive to, when they seek to discern the significance of the Bible for them? Such questions and many others could be explored now at mealtime at home, at the pubs or the places where women gathered to wash the laundry, just as one imagined the people of Galilee would have when they had listened to the Jew, Jesus of Nazareth.

I set aside the importance of his translation of the Bible for the German language; instead I pick up one effect of his 1523 pamphlet *That Jesus Christ Was Born a Jew*, and I have already alluded to it. For me this is the "and yet . . ." dimension of Luther's legacy for Jewish-Christian relations. Josel of Rosenheim had been taken aback by how the most precious word of Christianity, "Jesus Christ," came together in Luther's treatise with one that for many centuries was one of its most despised words, "Jew." Something dialogical opened up. Luther spoke with sympathy of his fellow-humans who deserved to be treated humanely. (The Nazis were not the initiator of the depiction of Jews as "subhuman." It was a deep and ancient cultural bias.) Luther drew on his reading of the Bible, in particular the prophets. It is true that Luther did not think that he should invite Josel to do exegesis of biblical texts together. However, the possibility that such joint Bible study might result was in the air. My own experience of the meetings of the Society of Biblical Literature tells me that most people who do biblical exegesis and interpretation today are persuaded that in order to be fruitful, it can be done only with Jews and Christians together. Christians today realize the necessity of bringing "home" Jesus *the Jew* just as much as Jews are ready to bring Jesus "home" as really one of their own. The fact that Jesus is Jewish has finally become a determinative factor in how the Second Testament is read and interpreted. Renaming the Old Testament into the "Hebrew Bible" is more than a concession to interfaith encounter. It is the acknowledgment of the firm ground on which Christian faith exists.

I conclude with words of Rabbi Albert Friedlander. He had composed a letter addressed to the Martin Luther of the sixteenth century. In it, he calls him Brother Martin from Eisleben, and tells him that he had salvaged that firm ground for Christianity's self-understanding even though he, Friedlander, has to struggle with Luther in order not to lose his own place. He concludes that they, Albert and Martin, are both children of Abraham, and that they have taken so many riches into their lives as a common inheritance that every idea and every word creates a link between them. Indeed, they share the same hope for the end of time. But there was one thing that he had to ask of Luther before concluding, because dark, hopeless times will come again, he implores:

> *Please, Martin, lock the door to the chamber of horrors that you had opened! Let it never come open again! And teach your followers that there are times when dogmas need to make room for human sympathy. For we are human beings and may not make God's judgment our own. Reaffirm for your followers that we are human beings and can love one another. May God protect us and bring us together, now and for all time.*[3]

May that blessing and admonition be a constant guide to our feet on the journey of the living tradition of the Reformation.

BIBLIOGRAPHY

Friedlander, Albert. "Jüdischer Glaube nach Auschwitz." In *Das Schweigen der Christen und die Menschlichkeit Gottes: Gläubige Existenz nach Auschwitz,* 37-52. Munich: Chr. Kaiser Verlag, 1990.
Wenschkewitz, Leonore-Siegele. "Josel von Rosenheim: Juden und Christen im Zeitalter der Reformation." *Kirche und Israel* 6 (1991): 3-16.

---

3. These lines are based in Albert Friedlander's essay, "Jüdischer Glaube nach Auschwitz," in *Das Schweigen der Christen und die Menschlichkeit Gottes: Gläubige Existenz nach Auschwitz* (Munich: Chr. Kaiser Verlag, 1990), 37-52.

11

The Death and Resurrection of God
The Story in a Post-Christian World
Donald F. Murray

As we honor Martin Luther and his impact on five hundred years of evolving theology, we also look forward to the next five hundred years, and the transformation now taking place that will make it possible. I think of W.B. Yeats' poem, "The Second Coming" (1921), in which he wrote, "Things fall apart/the center cannot hold/Mere anarchy is loosed upon the world." Yeats foretells that "Surely some revelation is at hand" and wonders "what rough beast . . . Slouches towards Bethlehem to be born?"[1] The poets knew long before the rest of us that something fundamental is changing. The "rough beast" is my theme here. We will continually meet some version of this, so the more we know about it, the better. In this chapter, I offer a glimpse of current material, spiritual, and historical realities as we can now understand them, and explore the implications for religion.

THE TIMES THEY ARE A-CHANGIN'

It is not news to say that we live in changing times. Understanding the magnitude of the change, and integrating it into our thinking and living, is the challenge. The moment and circumstances in which we now find ourselves

---

1. Yeats, "The Second Coming."

are the result of approximately 13.8 billion years of the universe's evolution, a vast period. In terms of earth's geological ages, we are moving from the sixty five million year old Cenozoic era to what Thomas Berry and Brian Swimme describe as the Ecozoic era.[2] Humans now dictate the future of the earth. It is an awesome responsibility.

There are many ways to look at the transformation that is now happening. Our time has been called the second Axial Age. The first such Age (circa 800 to 300 BCE), brought to human awareness the values that make us human.[3] In Israel, it was the prophets of the eighth to fourth century. "Do justice . . . love kindness . . . walk humbly" (Mic 6:8), covers a lot of ground. In our present age, the law written in the heart (Jer 31:33) requires us to live out the values that were brought to consciousness in that ancient period, lest we suffer the agonies of the book of Revelation. A giant leap in consciousness and maturity is required. We are also moving from the astrological age of Pisces to the age of Aquarius. Pisces began near the time of Jesus' birth and ends about now. Pisces was the age of moving from heaven to earth, from the supernatural to the psychological, and the emerging of the individual. Aquarius represents the age of an earthy spirituality, the emergence of the psyche, and a focus on community. To enter Aquarius requires us to live the qualities unearthed in the first Axial Age, or face dire consequences. Can we make the giant leap in consciousness and avoid our own demise?

When Copernicus gazed into the heavens and concluded that the earth is not the center of the universe, the age of supernatural religion as a creative force in advancing consciousness was over. During the course of the last five hundred years, the Newtonian paradigm—rationality, the scientific method, and a clockwork universe—has taken over the secular Western mind. Such a universe has no room for God. This reality broke into the consciousness of the church in the "death-of-God" theology of the 1960s.[4] In that decade, there was little language to speak about this experience of the "death of God." Dietrich Bonhoeffer was a comfort and guide for me during those years. In the flood of insights that poured forth from his prison letters of April 30, 1944, and after, especially those written to his friend Eberhart Bethge, he became aware of issues with which we still wrestle. "What is Christianity, and indeed what is Christ for us today? . . . We are

---

2. Swimme and Berry, *The Universe Story*.
3. Armstrong, *The Great Transformation*.
4. For more on this, see Irion, *From the Ashes of Christianity*.

Living Traditions

proceeding toward a time of no religion at all . . . God is being pushed out of the world." He also believed that "the day will come when [people] will be called upon to utter the word of God with such power as will change and renew the world. It will be a new language."[5] That day might not yet be here, but we are learning the language.

The social upheaval of the 1960s marked the death of traditional religions in the collective consciousness of the Western soul, especially for the Caucasian population of Western Europe, the USA, and Canada. The exodus from the church began and has continued. The "old, old, story" no longer grasps contemporary minds. The recent controversy in The United Church of Canada over local church minister Gretta Vosper and her anti-theistic stance has its roots in the 1960s. She is bearing eloquent witness to a reality to which we need to pay attention.

WHERE ARE WE?

As M.T. Winter said at a recent gathering of the Atlantic Seminar in Theological Education in Truro, Nova Scotia, "When an old story dies, a new and larger one is being born."[6] This is happening now. The fading out of traditional religions is bringing about a spiritual awakening. With the death of the old, all kinds of spiritualities are being explored. Eastern religions have brought solace to many. Yoga has swept through the West, with its emphasis on body, mind, and spirit. All are signs of spiritual unrest and yearning.

We are also in the midst of a shift from a Newtonian paradigm to a quantum paradigm. Two towering minds of the twentieth century, along with many followers, have made this possible. Albert Einstein (1879–1955) triggered the scientific evolution from Newtonian science to quantum science. In 1907, in his spare time from the patent office, he wrote a paper on the theory of special relativity. As a result, the universe has once again become a place of wonder and mystery. The Hubble telescope, among other technological advances, has extended human sight to the far reaches of this vast, beautiful, and mysterious, universe.

The other paradigm is that of Carl Jung (1875–1961).[7] I would argue that he is also one of the transforming minds of the contemporary

---

5. Bonhoeffer, *Prisoner for God*, 121, 140.
6. Winter, as transcribed in the author's notes.
7. See Jung, *Memories, Dreams, Reflections*.

world. Born into a clergy family in 1875, he transformed traditional understandings of Christianity and all religious language, moving from an emphasis on supernatural language to the language of the psyche or soul. This is perhaps the new language of which Bonhoeffer spoke. Jung's break with Sigmund Freud occurred about the same time as Einstein was writing his famous papers. It marks Jung's plunge into the depths and mystery of the psyche, both individual and universal. Religious language becomes psychic language, relating us to our own depths and to the realities of archetypes and the psychic world.

Einstein re-presented the material universe in a remarkable way. Jung offered new insights into the psychic universe. Our bodies find their home in the material universe. Sallie McFague has in fact called the material universe the "body of God."[8] The material universe operates and evolves according to its own rules, even as our bodies function in their own wondrous ways, largely apart from our awareness. We do well, then, to give careful attention to our minds, our psyches, our consciousness, and our souls—all of which express who we are—and to live life through our bodies. Our bodies are the vehicles for our psyches, our souls. The wider psychic or soul universe in which we participate lives out its intent through the material universe, just as we live out our intent through our bodies.

Thomas Berry named this emerging story the "universe story."[9] The universe, in its material and non-material dimensions, has evolved us as creatures with self-reflective awareness. We have come from the earth and the universe. We are the universe seeing itself. We are the universe hearing itself. We are the universe intuiting itself. As the *Desiderata* phrase says, "you are a child of the universe." This is our emerging story. As we meditate on the universe, in all its wonder and beauty, and on our souls as reflections of the heart and soul of the universe, the universe story is gradually taking on a numinous quality and truly becoming our story. It is the resurrection of God. But the universe story is nothing new. It is the age-old story that has ever been with us. The first step into becoming human, some four million years ago, took place when some female creature stood on her hind legs, looked up at the stars and said, "Wow, what's that all about?" We now know a great deal more about the universe, but it still engenders awe.

---

8. McFague, *The Body of God*.
9. Swimme and Berry, *The Universe Story*.

Living Traditions

IMPLICATIONS FOR RELIGION

As human history unfolds, we find ourselves sitting around the conference table in the Global Village. Science and technology have brought us here. The present wave of countries moving toward exclusion and isolation demonstrates that the need for progress and unity, which is obvious to some, is not embraced by all. Trying to go back to a prior age is a priority for others. Many things bind us together into one human family, yet we are only beginning to evolve a coherent and compelling story that will form us into one people. In this quest, no traditional religion can claim universality. We all have partial stories that are divisive in their extreme forms. The universe story (as presented by Swimme and Berry) offers us a universal mythology that draws us together as children, or adults, of the universe. Rites, rituals, and liturgies, therefore, need to be focused around the universe story. Anecdotally, I note an increase in references to earth, universe, and cosmic images in the context of worship. Walter Murray (my brother) occasionally leads worship at a little country church, where they sit in a circle for worship and gaze up at a ceiling studded with stars.

Any new insight, movement, or religion grows out of what has gone before, and adds a new dimension to the human view of reality. The images of death and resurrection are appropriate. The old is not lost, but is transformed into a larger new body. Over the eons, religions and cultures have emerged and died. They have been major forces in pushing and pulling us forward on our journey to be fully human. It would be tragic to lose touch with the religions that are fading. However, we see them now in a new light. For many in the contemporary West, they are no longer pathways to the Holy. Rather, they offer us the wisdom gained through the ages, and a profound connection with our evolving history. As we move into a new era, we find special wisdom in the religion that formed each of us. Those from a Christian background will find that the Bible holds special interest. Since consciousness and learning how to be human are what life is all about, I would argue that that the Bible is the best witness the Western world has to the evolution of consciousness. From Eve's first step into consciousness, to the new heaven and the new earth of Revelation, it is a magnificent story. It presents us with the profound wisdom of a history-shaping tradition.

CONCLUSION: THE COSMIC WOMAN

I close with a powerful mythic image from the book of Revelation, which is indeed a most relevant book for our time. The image of the "cosmic woman" provides a clue to understanding Revelation, the Bible, and indeed, the whole human venture:

> A great portent appeared in heaven: a woman, clothed with the sun, with the moon under her feet, and on her head a crown of twelve stars (Rev 12:1).

This is the ultimate, archetypal woman of the universe, the one called Sophia in the book of Proverbs, in all her cosmic glory. She is the creative power of the universe, the goddess in her fullness.

> She was pregnant and was crying out in birth pangs, in the agony of giving birth . . . And she gave birth to a . . . child, who is to rule all the nations with a rod of iron (Rev 12:2,5).

There are endless discussions over whom or what the child represents, and the language of "ruling with a rod of iron" makes the picture still more complex. For my purposes here and for our present moment in history, I would argue that the child identified here is humankind in its glorious wholeness. The universe (the cosmic woman) is struggling to bring forth a fully conscious and mature humanity. That is what is needed for human survival. Even so, there is more to the story:

> Then another portent appeared in heaven: a great red dragon, with seven heads and ten horns, and seven diadems on his heads . . . Then the dragon stood before the woman who was about to bear a child, so that he might devour her child as soon as it was born (Rev 12:3-4).

It is a horrific image, but this dragon represents the reality of the contemporary world. We are faced with many "red dragons" today, including political regimes in which oppression and terror threaten the wholeness of life for millions. The forces of evil are powerful and ubiquitous. They represent the measure of human immaturity. Many have struggled with personal "dragons" as well as those afoot in the world. However, Richard Rubenstein suggests that history works out its own justice, even though it is a long road.[10] Martin Luther King Jr. is famously remembered to have restated

---

10. Rubenstein, *The Cunning of History*.

abolitionist Theodore Parker's hopeful assertion that "The arc of the moral universe is long, but it bends towards justice."

With the resurgence of the "red dragons," we must prepare ourselves for a new dark age, knowing that, like John, the author of the book of Revelation, we will need courage and endurance. On the far side awaits the new heaven and new earth. The new/old universe story is an elegant "beast," rushing—not slouching—"towards Bethlehem to be born." That story will help us make the great transition.

BIBLIOGRAPHY

Armstrong, Karen. *The Great Transformation: The Beginning of our Religious Traditions.* Toronto: Knopf Canada, 2006.

Bonhoeffer, Dietrich. *Prisoner for God: Letters and Papers from Prison.* Edited by Eberhard Bethge. Translated by Reginald H. Fuller. New York: MacMillan, 1954.

Irion, Mary Jean. *From the Ashes of Christianity: A Post-Christian View.* New York: J. B. Lipincott, 1968.

Jung, C.G. *Memories, Dreams, Reflections.* Edited by Aniela Jaffe. Translated by Richard and Clara Winston. New York: Vantage, 1989.

McFague, Sallie. *The Body of God: An Ecological Theology.* Minneapolis: Augsburg, 1993.

Rubinstein, Richard L. *The Cunning of History: Mass Death and the American Future.* New York: Harper & Row, 1975.

Swimme, Brian, and Thomas Berry. *The Universe Story: From the Primordial Flaring Forth to the Ecozoic Era, A Celebration of the Unfolding of the Cosmos.* New York: Harper, 1992.

Yeats, W.B. "The Second Coming." https://www.poetryfoundation.org/poems/43290/the-second-coming.

12

Literary Imagination and Theology
Protestant and Catholic Response to *The Lord of the Rings*
Allen B. Robertson

FIVE HUNDRED YEARS AFTER the beginning of the Protestant Reformation inspired by Martin Luther, we are in a position to examine both the distinct differences and commonalities between Reform religion and the enduring Catholic Church. It is my intent to use the medium of fantasy literature to illustrate divergences and intersections of thought, specifically, Protestant and Catholic response to J.R.R. Tolkien's *The Lord of the Rings*, as encountered primarily in literary text, with some observations on the Peter Jackson film trilogy based on the same.

Interpretation of imaginative literature, once it has left the private preserve of an author and been made available to the general public, is subject to the varied background of each reader. The additional interplay of religious considerations in response to fiction can be arrayed in potentially opposing viewpoints between Protestant and Roman Catholic doctrinal bases. One significant example has been reaction to Tolkien's best-known fantasy creation. It is the product of an extraordinary imagination, while at the same time it is the expression of a lay Catholic theologian whose faith is infused within the text. Tolkien was predominantly shaped by a Thomist theology and philosophy in his religious upbringing.[1] Protestant scholars on reviewing *The Lord of the Rings* tend to be grounded in Augustinian theology of the late patristic age. Thomas Aquinas, by contrast, was the epitome of the late medieval Catholic theological synthesis, fitting, perhaps, for Tolkien's quasi-medieval saga. It does raise the question of how Protestant readers can engage with *The Lord of the Rings* text once they recognize Tolkien's substrata of Catholicism and his own theological insights.[2] Common ground, degrees of hesitancy, and judgement may be considered in comparison with scholars who have employed Catholic spirituality in assessing Tolkien's writing. This study seeks to discern if a rapprochement of theologies is in evidence over the sixty years since *The Lord of the Rings* appeared in print.[3]

Does Tolkien's writing advocate salvation by works? For some reviewers this is a critical point, for it touches on the Protestant legacy of the relationship between faith and good works. The level of didactic reference to the Christian faith similarly has been a subject of consideration—not only for Tolkien's writing, but also for the field of literature and artistic creation in general. Awareness of Catholic motifs within *The Lord of the Rings* has at times generated some disquiet over the impact these motifs might have on impressionable readers who are not Catholic.[4]

Finding a starting point for discussion may lie in the aforementioned stance on the validity of literary imagination in general and fantasy writing in particular. It has been argued that from the Protestant perspective, the focus is on the message created out of writing, where the latter is the tool and the former is the spiritual goal. Catholicism, on the other hand, has seen creativity itself as a spiritual engagement through utilizing the gifts bestowed by the Creator. C.S. Lewis's *The Lion, The Witch and The Wardrobe* and subsequent *Chronicles of Narnia* novels (1950-56) are overtly Christian

---

1. Robertson, "Voices in Tolkien." See also Kreeft, *Philosophy of Tolkien*.

2. Protestant scholars have engaged in that discussion. See Imbert, *"Who Invented the Stories Anyway?"*

3. Tolkien's work was initially published as three separate books, the first appearing in 1954 (*The Lord of the Rings: The Fellowship of the Ring*), followed by *The Two Towers* and *The Return of the King* in 1955.

4. One may suspend commentary on more extreme approaches (Protestant or Catholic) that reject all forms of fantasy and the imaginary world of magic and spirits, whether coming out of general myth and folklore or the later fairy-story genre. "In a tradition steeped in the primacy of the written word and spoken word, many Protestants were apprehensive about the lure of images, icons, and other forms of Catholic material culture that were designed to engage the senses." Payne, "Roman Catholicism," 421.

in content and message. Indeed, biblical literacy enhances the meanings attached to the images used, such as Aslan's sacrifice and resurrection. General knowledge of Protestant literature, such as Bunyan's *The Pilgrim's Progress* (1678), would shed further light on Lewis's series. J.R.R. Tolkien, whose idea of sub-creation has its roots in the doctrine of being made in the likeness and image of God, shares in the Catholic idea that to create is a spiritual exercise, since it is to participate in the divine gift of creativity. The distinction between the overt and subliminal has been pointed out by Kath Filmer-Davies: "Lewis, of course, writes polemically: he knew the tactics of argument, dialectic and rhetoric, and he exercised his skill throughout the entire range of his writing." Filmer-Davies continues, arguing, "Tolkien, on the other hand, used fantasy more covertly; religious themes are to be found in his best-known work *The Lord of the Rings*, but they operate almost subversively, without distracting from the autotelic nature of the quest epic itself."[5] On that basis, *The Lord of the Rings* is set in a pre-incarnation age without direct evocation of Christian imagery or ritual. The author's own faith emerges in certain themes and indirect allusions that avoid the didactic literary approach of his contemporary Lewis.

A common resonance can be found in references in *The Lord of the Rings* to the inherent beauty of the natural world and in creativity itself, whether that be poetic language to describe trees, flowers, mountains, and other natural wonders; or the appreciation of manuscripts as physical objects of art; the architecture of the dwarfs, elves, hobbits, and humans; and free flowing interchange between poetry and song. The natural world as indicative of God's creation has been long appreciated in Protestant literature. One might quote the Canadian province of Nova Scotia's eighteenth century, evangelical author Henry Alline (1748-1784), who in his hymns and poems, as well as his spiritual journal, recapitulates the encounter with God by way of his handiworks, as shown in *A Universal Song*:

> Awake thou bell'wing ocean wide,
> Rouse all the tenants of your deeps
> And let the murmur of your tide,
> Boil up, and his praises leap.
> Ye cragged rocks around the main,
> And fragrant flow'rs of ev'ry hue,
> With the tall cedars of the plains

---

5. Filmer-Davies, *Scepticism*, 22-3. See also Patrick, "J. R. R. Tolkien," 82-6.

Living Traditions

> All join to praise your maker too.[6]

Comparatively recent ecological stewardship, which has entered theological writings in Protestantism and Catholicism, can likewise find attachment to Tolkien's respect for balance in the world and his antithetical descriptions of wanton technological disruption (whether a polluting mill in the Shire or Saruman's smokes and poisoned waters at Orthanc). One can find, of course, a precedent of literary critique of industrial blight in Charles Dickens's *Hard Times*. Not to be forgotten, though, is the analogy of a blight on the soul and attempts to discourage imagination (in Dickens's character, Mr. Gradgrind), just as Tolkien's depiction of Saruman's armories bespeak of a departure from the enriching gifts of creation. The English mystic William Blake encapsulated both aspects in the first stanza of *Jerusalem*:

> And did those feet in ancient time
> Walk upon England's mountains green?
> And was the holy Lamb of God
> On England's pleasant pastures seen?
> And did the countenance divine
> Shine forth upon our clouded hills?
> And was Jerusalem builded here
> Among those dark satanic mills?[7]

Blake might be considered unorthodox in his beliefs, yet his vibrant, imaginative lines entered into popular piety in defiance of residual Puritanism.

Fallenness in Tolkien's broader literary creations, including *The Lord of the Rings*, does allude to Edenic loss and the quest for restoration.[8] In this there is tension between the Catholic position as transmitted by way of Aquinas through Tolkien, insofar as the Fall is said to have not totally effaced the *imago dei*. Classic Protestantism through Calvin and Knox taught the utter depravity of humankind after the Fall as one way of emphasizing the complete dependence on the mercy of God in the act of salvation. It is this visionary divergence that has led some Protestant scholars and reviewers to express a degree of discomfort with *The Lord of the Rings*. There have been attempts to balance Tolkien's basic Thomism with Augustinianism, notably in how Augustine described the nature of evil as the wounding

---

6. Alline, *Hymns and Spiritual Songs*, 384-5.
7. *Traditional* Hymns, 153.
8. Robertson, "Two Paths to Joy," 20-31.

of the good. Robert Koons, in his review of Baptist scholar Ralph Wood's *The Gospel According to Tolkien,* first elaborates Wood's understanding of Catholicism as applied to a reading of *The Lord of the Rings* before highlighting how Tolkien, "with St. Paul and Augustine, sees the power of evil lying in its capacity to enslave the will itself."[9] The One Ruling Ring is the embodiment of that danger. The contrast lies in Tolkien's adhering to Aquinas in allowing for a residual of the human will that survived the Fall. That is, the will may be wounded, but the creation of God cannot be wholly overwhelmed without the active participation of the creature to reject the Good. Whereas Reform faith wanted to emphasis the complete reliance on God for all things and to counter any residual influence of Pelagianism, one finds in Catholicism the idea that the essential inner spark of the divine exists both as a base from which the will can position itself to accept or reject grace. It is this spark that is drawn to its ultimate source, the sole life-giving flame of the universe, the innate Love who is God.[10]

Tolkien's reference to the Secret Fire can be seen as an evocation of the Holy Spirit that animates creation. The will that allows itself to be fed by the *imago dei* (or the inner fire) can achieve much, yet the necessity of God is not overthrown. Koons sees adherence to this belief as the rejection of Pelagianism insofar as Tolkien allows Frodo to finally "fail" at the Crack of Doom. Frodo's prior expression of the virtues nonetheless saved him because he allowed Providence to intervene during acts of mercy and *caritas* toward Gollum.[11] This is a bridge between strict Calvinism and Thomism. In the end it is the grace of God that must aid one to achieve salvation, "for the spirit is willing but the flesh is weak."

Nature and grace come in for a delicate balancing in the narrative of *The Lord of the Rings.* Christian spirituality orients one toward contemplation of the Divine while the material world recedes in significance. Acts of charity toward others in this world are manifestations of a dynamic inner working between the soul and God. Joseph Komonchak explains this as an Augustinian clarity and spareness of doctrinal understanding.[12] Thomism, by contrast, without denying the centrality of God, does not perceive na-

---

9. Koons, "A Baptist Perspective," 34-8.

10. Augustine did not teach utter depravity. He still saw the goodness of God enduring even divine judgement, for if the former held, then there would have been utter annihilation of the creature. See Augustine, *An Augustine Reader,* 420.

11. Birzer, *J. R. R. Tolkien's Sanctifying Myth.*

12. Komonchak, "A Postmodern Augustinian Thomism?", 123-46.

ture as essentially negligible even if one were to express God's providence in evocative literary expression as an Augustinian. Nature is the place wherein we exist in space and time, and is the platform from which to actualize the unleashing of the spiritual potential of each person.[13] Moreover, though likewise wounded in the Fall, nature retains the impress of God's creative intervention (as does the *imago dei* in humankind). To regard the material world as reflections of the Good is to acknowledge that origin and its kinship to the human soul. Corruption of nature—whether in the natural world or in persons within it—is abhorrent in that it is the marring of the vestiges of the Good. Hence the ruined landscapes near the gates of Mordor are an assault on the original intentions of Eru (the One). The ruination of Orcs, and half-man/half-orcs (the Uruk-hai), denies the *imago dei*.[14]

Rolland Hein states that, "We intellectualize in order to know, but paradoxically, intellectualization tends to destroy its object. The harder we grasp at the thing, the more its reality moves away."[15] He goes on to say that imagination can override this dilemma through, among other forms, expression in images, gestures, and symbols, with the culmination in myths. Here one crosses over into Tolkien's territory—fantasy literature—in which semiotic impasses are leapt over in order to explore human nature and divine presence. Hein beautifully illustrates this point in referring to William Blake, when a friend asked if he saw only an object of light when the sun rose: "'Oh no, I see an immeasurable company of the heavenly host crying, 'Holy, Holy is the Lord God Almighty.'"[16] In *On Fairy Stories*, Tolkien took these ideas further by concluding that imagination—by way of what he came to call sub-creation—was inherent: "Fantasy remains a human right: we make in our measure and in our derivative mode, because we are made: and not only made, but made in the image and likeness of a Maker." This is not a usurpation of the role of Creator; it is the impulse of humankind to manifest creativity as innate and vital in recognizing that the ability to do so derives from the First Cause or God. The success or failure of literary

---

13. Komonchak, ibid. A detailed discussion of Aquinas and nature can be found in Konyndyk DeYoung *et al., Aquinas's Ethics*.

14. Lewis struggled with aspects of nature and grace, as seen in a letter concerning his book *That Hideous Strength*: "I think That Hideous Strength is about a triple conflict: Grace against Nature and Nature against Anti-Nature (modern industrialization, scientism and totalitarian politics)." Lewis, cited Pearce, *Catholic Literary* Greats, 55.

15. Hein, *Christian Mythmakers*, x.

16. Ibid., xiii.

expression, from the Christian perspective, depends on whether it moves toward the Good or away from it.

In his examination of literature and the fantasy genre, Lee Oser aligns Tolkien with Chesterton and Eliot as indicative of the struggle against modernity.[17] One acute observation brings to the fore a substantial contrast between Catholic and Protestant authors. The former live as a matter of course with the wondrous by way of eucharistic teaching.[18] During the Mass one encounters the sign and the "thing itself," the transformative means by which Christ incorporates us into himself to be offered to and drawn up into the Father.[19] Protestant teaching, having abandoned transubstantiation, moved into the realm of sign and heightened spiritual awareness. The distinction, however, distanced the worshipper from immanence. Sacrament shifted in some denominations to ordinances, which vacated the numinous from the assembly. This theological pathway further influenced emerging Protestant sensibilities in the realm of imaginative writing, and by extension, fantasy, as the latter developed in the nineteenth century. Tales of wizards, magic, and fantasy beings become distractions at best and agents of diabolism at worst. The caveat certainly must be that Protestantism is a spectrum. Statements on literary imagination and Protestant response likewise need to be elastic in their application. High Church Anglicanism is closer to Catholic understandings of the eucharistic Presence than to evangelical Methodism. British dissenters are more open to liberal ideas than Fundamentalists of the United States.[20]

One likewise might speak of Catholicism in general terms, yet within the greater body there are varieties of pious practice, social-public engagement, and theological camps of conservatives and liberals. Individuals can partake of a mix of all these variants. Reference to Tolkien's Thomist position must accommodate certain Augustinian viewpoints that Tolkien

---

17. Oser, *Return of Christian Humanism*.

18. "At root, the metaphysical assumptions of Catholicism differ from those of English Protestantism. Coleridge and the romantic movement are, in consequence, forced to steal the power of heaven, while Catholics are at home in a world of sacramental miracles. The romantic imagination is militant; the Catholic imagination is daring." Oser, *Return of Christian Humanism*, 58.

19. "J. R. R. Tolkien was a Catholic who had traditional Catholicism, the Catholicism of altars, feasts, fasts, heroic suffering, rituals, saints, miracles, doctrines, and mysteries in his very bones." Craven, "Catholic Poem in Time of War."

20. See Worthen, "John Stott."

embraced.[21] Core unity does exist to the extent that the permeability of the liturgy, which allows for transcendence in the moment, permitted Tolkien by analogy to blend pagan inspired myths and Christian virtues.[22] Tolkien's world was centered on the Eucharist. From this orientation he developed his themes of sub-creation, incarnation, resurrection, and eucatastrophe.

The Gospel, radiating outward into the rest of scripture, fixes Protestantism's focus on Christ, the Word of Life. It is the only true story. Tolkien's sub-creation and eucatastrophe did not deny that belief: he called it a "true myth." Yet he allowed that it radiated into reality and time spreading glimpses into human minds before and since the resurrection of Jesus.[23] There is a similar teaching in Augustine, who in *The City of God* wrote that Christ's redemption and resurrection saved righteous persons of past ages.[24] Pagan myths or metaphysical narratives of other faith traditions of the past all received in partial measure some of this splintered light. This idea validated preservation of oral and written inheritances from the past, for these stories hinted at *imago dei* and true myth. Luther spoke of *sola scriptura*. Tolkien in his writings studied words with their origins and inherent mythic content, used words in fantasy creation, and unreservedly believed in the Word as proclaimed in the opening of St. John's gospel.

Protestants and Catholics diverge and cross over their understandings of the Word, and neither relinquish the generative beingness of Word as God's unfolding of reality. Tolkien's cosmological myth, which opens *The Silmarillion* and is the greater context for *The Lord of the Rings*, speaks poetically of the One (Eru) conceiving musical themes through the Vala—themes that are given substance as Middle-Earth. Throughout *The Lord of the Rings*, music as song or natural sound (especially water) reiterates the greater music of creation. Words as echoes of the Word can as a consequence sparkle with creative radiance in accordance with Tolkien's idea of sub-creation. Chris Armstrong perceives literature as one means for conveying the Word in his commentary on Tolkien:

---

21. Oser, *Return of Christian Humanism*, 59. See also Birzer, "St. Augustine and J. R. R. Tolkien" and Yulo, "The Temptation of the Earthly City."

22. "It is a poem that under the two great passions of Tolkien's life, Northern Germanic mythology . . . and the sacramental mysteries of the Catholic Church." Craven, "Catholic Poem in Time of War."

23. "Tolkien's belief that God in his grace has prefigured the gospel *evangelism* in human stories, a view shared by C. S. Lewis, was a kind of natural theology." Duriez, *Tolkien and The Lord of the Rings*, 198.

24. Augustine, *An Augustine Reader*, 473.

> Whether each reader is willing to accept the echoes of that Greater Myth in the "new myth" that came from Tolkien's pen has much to do—I am convinced—with whether they are able to perceive and receive God's grace in the stuff of culture. Do they see God present not only in the ordained elements of bread and wine at the altar but also in the "everyday sacraments" of books, conversations, music, art?[25]

That step is essential in order to let in the light into our mundane existence. It bolsters our communal participation in worship, reading of scripture, and other explicit expressions of Christianity. Sometimes an overly scrupulous conscience can lead to missed opportunities for glimmers of immanence.

Reference was made earlier in this essay to Bunyan's *The Pilgrim's Progress*, a highly colored allegory of the Christian path through life to the fullness of life. Doctrine, virtues, and temptations were all personified with self-evident names. Two and a half centuries later, J.R.R. Tolkien likewise wrote about a journey that can be called a pilgrim passage. His narrative, however, exemplified virtues in character traits in accordance with Thomist teaching: Prudence, Justice, Fortitude, Temperance, in alliance with the three theological virtues of Faith, Hope, and Love. All are means to conform one's life in the journey toward and union with the Good. Tolkien fused Christian understanding as a subtext in *The Lord of the Rings*. The four cardinal and three theological virtues resonate with the original teaching of Christ, ripple through time to Augustine and the writings of St. Thomas Aquinas, and are refracted in the reform teachings of Luther and his contemporaries while then passing to the inheritance of Bunyan and C.S. Lewis as they composed their literary works to convey the gospel and teach the virtues. Tolkien took the gift of creative imagination (that is, sub-creation) to provide flesh in which the spirit animated the virtues and looked forward to the redemption of both nature and spirit. He did not advocate salvation by works. Rather, one works out the reality of spirit wrestling in the now through the great eucatastrophes of the incarnation and the resurrection. In that sense, the Word that was in the beginning (and was neither Protestant nor Catholic) can be heard in literary imagination in general and in Christian fantasy in particular, such as *The Lord of the Rings*.

It would be remiss to omit the foremost film adaptation of Tolkien's major writing by Peter Jackson. The film version of *The Lord of the Rings* has

---

25. Armstrong, "Saint J. R. R. the Evangelist." See also McAvan, *The Postmodern Sacred* and Morrow, "J. R. R. Tolkien and C. S. Lewis."

renewed discussion of the original text along with the new visual incarnation. "Adaptation" is the key here, for as true devotees know, much has been omitted and certain so-called improvements have been introduced. Does the redacted film offer any glimmer of Tolkien's message and the underlying Catholic imagery? Like the music of J.S. Bach, which survives many adaptations of instrumentation while retaining its original inspiration, so too Tolkien's writing in its transmigration to film still permits virtues to be illuminated.[26] The figure of Galadriel has not wholly lost allusions to Our Lady, nor has *lembas* been utterly stripped of it eucharistic imagery. Justice and mercy toward Gollum foretell the gift of grace offered to Frodo when his mortal frame and spirit cannot complete the task of casting the Ring into Orodruin's fiery furnace. The unexpected happy ending, which Tolkien had lectured on and then used to develop his concept of eucatastrophe, finds its place in the overthrow of Sauron.

Indirect evidence of film viewers turning to the original Tolkien book to further explore the movie's premise can be garnered from the mass republications of *The Lord of the Rings* on paper. Similarly (though of course quite different), hearing the Word of God was enhanced with the Reformation's making accessible the printed Bible in the language of the various peoples of Europe and beyond. Interpretation became the challenge, for once a book leaves the printer and is in the hands of readers, what is understood is in large measure determined by the background of those readers. Bunyan was overt in his writing to ensure that no one missed the point. C.S. Lewis mixed overt and nuanced literary devices for he knew too well that many were no longer as "churched" as once they had been, and perhaps had never been. Memorable characters, noble causes, love, sacrifice, endurance, and hope: these things Tolkien wove into his text to carry the virtues and to gain a glimpse of the Good, hoping that these might also be activated in the reader. His literary imagination carried the splintered light with hope for the future. It is reminiscent of the Jewish mystical teaching of the Zohar, wherein one of the central narratives speaks of the Light of Creation as having been carried in a bowl or vessels which broke and scattered throughout the world with sparks of light attached. Devoted sages (or all Jews) gather up the sparks so that one day the original whole of Creation may be restored.[27]

26. Catholic media devoted considerable coverage to the filmography and the text. See Pearce, "True Myth;" Greydanus, "From Book to Film;" Bittarello, "Review of Christopher Garbowski;" and Johnston, "Christian Theology."

27. This refers to the "shattering of the vessels" or "Shevirat haKeilim." See Schwartz, "How the Ari Created a Myth."

That is a creative, imaginative narrative with hope. Protestant and Catholic response to *The Lord of the Rings* speaks less of differences than of mutual meeting of spiritual legacies that may yet together recapture Tolkien's two great eucatastrophes in words spoken and written.

BIBLIOGRAPHY

Alline, Henry. *Hymns and Spiritual Songs*, 3rd ed. Dover, NH: Samuel Bragg, 1797.
Armstrong, Chris. "Saint J. R. R. the Evangelist," *Christianity Today* (1 Mar 2003). https://www.christianitytoday.com/ct/2003/marchweb-only/3-10-54.0.html
Augustine. *An Augustine Reader*. Edited by John J. O'Meara. Garden City, NY: Image, 1973.
Birzer, Bradley J. *J. R. R. Tolkien's Sanctifying Myth: Understanding Middle-Earth*. N.p: ISI Books, 2002.
———. "St. Augustine and J. R. R. Tolkien." *The Imaginative Conservative* (3 Feb 2011). https://theimaginativeconservative.org/2011/01/st-augustine-and-hopefully-someday-st.html.
Bittarello, Maria Beatrice. "Review of Christopher Garbowski, *Spiritual Values in Peter Jackson's The Lord of the Rings*." *Journal of Religion and Popular Culture* 16, no.1 (Summer 2007): 6.
Craven, Ken. "Catholic Poem in Time of War: The Lord of the Rings," Catholic Education Resource Centre, https://www.catholiceducation.org/en/culture/art/catholic-poem-in-time-of-war-the-lord-of-the-rings.html.
Duriez, Colin. *Tolkien and The Lord of the Rings: A Guide to Middle Earth*. London: Hidden Spring, 2001.
Filmer-Davies, Kath. *Scepticism and Hope in Twentieth Century Fantasy Literature*. Bowling Green, OH: Bowling Green State University Press, 1992.
Greydanus, Steven D. "From Book to Film: Will Peter Jackson's film trilogy be faithful to Tolkien?" *Catholic World Report* (Dec 2001): 44-7.
Hein, Rolland. *Christian Mythmakers: C. S. Lewis, Madeleine L'Engle, J. R. R. Tolkien, George MacDonald, G. K. Chesterton, Charles Williams, Dante Alighieri, John Bunyan, Walter Wangerin, Robert Siegel, and Hannah Hurnard*, 2nd ed. Chicago: Cornerstone, 2002.
Imbert, Yannick F. *"Who invented the stories anyway?" A Reformed Perspective on Tolkien's Theory of Fantasy*. Glenside, PA: Westminster Theological Seminary, 2010.
Johnston, Kristin Kay. "Christian Theology as Depicted in *The Lord of the Rings* and the Harry Potter Books." *Journal of Religion & Society* 7 (2005): 1-9.
Komonchak, Joseph A. "A Postmodern Augustinian Thomism?" In *Augustine and Postmodern Thought: A New Alliance against Modernity?*, 123-46. Edited by L. Boeve, M. Lumberigts, and M. Wisse. Leuven: Peeters, 2009.
Konyndyk DeYoung, Rebecca, and Colleen McCluskey, and Christian Vandyke. *Aquinas's Ethics: Metaphysical Foundations, Moral Theory and Theological Context*. Notre Dame, IN: University of Notre Dame Press, 2009.
Koons, Robert C. "A Baptist Perspective on Tolkien's Catholic Evangelism: Review of Ralph C. Woods, *The Gospel According to Tolkien*." *The University Bookman* 44, no. 1 (Fall 2005): 34-8.

Kreeft, Peter. *The Philosophy of Tolkien: The Worldview Behind The Lord of the Rings*. San Francisco: Ignatius, 2005.

McAvan, Emily. *The Postmodern Sacred: Popular Culture Spirituality in the Science Fiction, Fantasy and Urban Fantasy Genres*. Jefferson, NC: McFarland, 2012.

Morrow, Jeffrey L. "J. R. R. Tolkien and C. S. Lewis in light of Hans Urs Von Balthasar." *Renascence* 56, no. 3 (Spr 2004): 181-96.

Oser, Lee. *The Return of Christian Humanism: Chesterton, Eliot, Tolkien, and the Romance of History*. Columbia, MO: University of Missouri Press, 2007.

Patrick, James. "J. R. R. Tolkien and the Literary Catholic Revival." *The Latin Mass* (Spr 1999): 82-6.

Payne, Rodger M. "Roman Catholicism." In *The Routledge Companion to Religion and Popular Culture*, 421. Edited by John C. Lyden and Eric Michael Mazur. London and New York: Routledge, 2015.

Pearce, Joseph. *Catholic Literary Greats: A Field Guide to the Catholic Literary Landscape*. San Francisco: Ignatius, 2005.

Pearce, Joseph. "True Myth: The Catholicism of *The Lord of the Rings*." *Catholic World Report* (Dec 2001): 34-8.

Robertson, Allen B. "Two Paths to Joy: C. S. Lewis and J. R. R. Tolkien on Joy and Eucatastrophe." In *Both Sides of the Wardrobe: C. S. Lewis, Theological Imagination, and Everyday Discipleship*, 20-31. Edited by Rob Fennell. Eugene, OR: Resource Publications, 2015.

———. "Voices in Tolkien: Aquinas, *The Lord of the Rings* and True Myth in the Twenty-First Century." MA Thesis: Atlantic School of Theology, Halifax, NS, 2017.

Schwartz, Howard. "How the Ari Created a Myth and Transformed Judaism." *Tikkun* (28 March 2011). https://www.tikkun.org/newsite/how-the-ari-created-a-myth-and-transformed-judaism.

Traditional Hymns. London: Ebury, 1996.

Worthen, Molly. "John Stott, C. S. Lewis, J. R. R. Tolkien: Why American Evangelicals Love the British." *Religion & Politics* (1 May 2012). https://religionandpolitics.org/2012/05/01/john-stott-c-s-lewis-j-r-r-tolkien-why-american-evangelicals-love-the-british/

Yulo, Jose. "The Temptation of the Earthly City: Tolkien's Augustinian Visions." *Ignatius Insight* (1 Feb 2006). http://www.ignatiusinsight.com/features2006/jyulo_tolkiencity_feb06.asp.